M000310807

Printed and Published in the United States of America by Lillian Prince Mitchell Publishing

ISBN 978-0-692-80947-1

First Edition. December 5, 2016

Dee Jollah,

I hope this book
makes you LOL!

William Prince

DEDICATION

This book is dedicated to my mother, my father, and my husband.

Ma: Thank you for setting an amazing example of what a wife and mother should be. Thank you for showing me how to love and support my better half. Thank you for actually living the life that you preached about. For thirty-two years, I watched you love my father in sickness and in health til' death did you part. I know it wasn't always easy, and now that I'm "for real grown," I'm looking forward to some more very real, very candid conversations about how you kept it all together. I love and appreciate you so much.

Daddy: Thank you for showing me the way a man should love me by the way you loved my mother. Thank you for showing up to every piano lesson, track meet, and basketball game even though I wasn't all that good at any of them. Whether I was first or last to cross the finish line, (often dead last) I could still hear you screaming from the stands as if I were a star. Thank you for carving out time, just for me, every Thursday to go grocery shopping. I know nothing made you madder than when I clipped the back of your ankle with the grocery cart, but you still allowed me to tag along because that was "our thing." Thank you for setting a standard that showed me the men in this book didn't deserve me because I was fearfully and wonderfully made. Thank you for loving me first, for laughing at my jokes, and for trusting me with keeping things together after you were gone. I love you.

My husband: Tim, thank you for exceeding every standard and expectation that my father set. Loving you is the easiest, most effortless thing I've ever had to do. It's just as natural as breathing for me. Thank you for being my MUCH better half. For having a pure heart in all you do and for wanting the very best for me and for us. Thank you for showing me the world and for giving me your all. Thank you for loving me the way you do and for making me smile like only you can. You are all I ever hoped for and more than I deserve. 'Til death do us part. I love you.

NOTE:

All names, locations, years, and descriptions have been changed to protect the innocent. In other words, don't try to sue me if you think this is about you.

INTRODUCTION

"Did you leave?" is all the text message said.

After excusing myself to go to the bathroom over an hour ago, my date is just now realizing that I left. That, in itself, is much more insulting than me walking out on the date in the first place. Any guilt I may have felt prior to this moment just left.

We were only one drink and half an appetizer into the evening when he was already on Story #3 about his ex, Ashley. I knew things weren't going to go well when he told me that she had earrings exactly like the ones I was wearing. (Let me point out that there are no beads or feathers on my earrings. I have on the most basic silver hoops you've ever seen.)

At that point I accepted that I was merely playing the role of the Rebound for the night, and any expectation I had for a wonderful first date began to vanish.

At first, I thought that I could be unfairly judging him, so I tested my theory to be sure.

I said, not so genuinely, "You should give her a call and tell her how you feel." Here was his chance to make things right. I thought that he would respond and say something along the lines of, "What?! Never. I'm here with you, with your cute self. I'm not thinking about that girl."

Instead, he responded, "You think so?" His question was drenched in hope. Before I could respond, he had already gotten her on the main line.

"Hello, Ashley… it's me."

This is unacceptable.

So there I was, sitting at the table, looking and feeling all kinds of stupid as I listened to him try to rekindle things with Ashley. I could hear her screaming through the phone and from what I could gather, Ashley wasn't having it. I found some solace in knowing that both he and I were being rejected that night.

Finally, I had enough. I excused myself from the table and told him I was headed to the bathroom. I wasn't sure if he heard me or even cared, but I immediately walked back outside, retrieved my car from valet, and headed home.

It only took him a full hour to realize that I was gone. Either he thought that the calamari really upset my stomach and I'd been in the bathroom for the last sixty minutes, or this man JUST finished begging and pleading with Ashley. I'm going to be honest with myself and go with Option #2.

When did dating get this brutal? I feel like it was just yesterday when I dumped my boyfriend before heading to college at Morgan State University because I knew, for sure, that I would meet my husband there.

But that didn't happen.

Then I told myself, "It's OK, girl. By twenty-five, you'll be out of school, married, and working on Book #1 and Baby #2."

Welp. Absolutely NONE of that happened. I'm not even sure that I finished undergrad by the time I was twenty-five, and you're reading Book #1 right now. (I'm thirty-three by the way.)

Year after year, my solid plan began to unravel before my very eyes. My friends, including the boyfriend I dumped before heading to greener pastures in college, were all getting engaged, jumping brooms, and having babies, and I was just going on one awful date after the other.

I remember being a naïve, nineteen-year-old girl with a two-page list of standards. He had to be fly, cute, tall, and funny just to name a few. By the time I hit my late twenties, the only thing "he" had to be was breathing.

Year thirty was now on the horizon, and since it's a scientific fact that women will actually combust into thirty small pieces if they're not married with children by then, I began to question if I was the issue. *"What am I doing wrong?"* I began to ask myself. My sister, Sonja, had assured me over a million times and during countless conversations that it wasn't me. She promised me that the guys I dated were just intimidated by all I had going on. (Yeah, I'm sure my 2007 Camry with three hubcaps made them feel uncomfortable.) If I was crying hard enough, she would pull out the big guns and comfort me by saying that she knew God had saved someone just for me. I was starting not to believe her, and I don't even think she believed herself.

It had gotten so bad I wasn't even praying for a Happily Ever After anymore. I would have been fine with a Happily for Six Months to a Year—just long enough for me to attend one wedding and not have to write in *"N/A"* on the plus one line. I was tired of telling people, "Yeah, things are going great. I just got a promotion, I'm house hunting and I volunteer regularly at a women's shelter."

Only for that to be followed-up with, "so, no boyfriend?" It was as if my accomplishments meant nothing because I didn't have a man.

So I kicked it into high gear, lowered some of those standards, and convinced myself that I was just "temporarily compromising." I ignored red flags, no matter how hard they flapped and waved in the wind, in hopes of finding true love faster. But all it led to was the kind of embarrassing and humbling moments that are only funny ten years later.

So let me tell you what happened.

Welcome to *10 Dates Later...*

1 Corinthians 13:11 International Standard Version:

When I was a child, I talked like a child, I thought like a child, I reasoned like a child.

Nineteen-Year-Old Lillian's Must-Have List

1. Fly (gotta keep a fresh pair of shoes)

2. Cute

3. Tall

4. Keeps a fresh haircut

5. Has a license and car (or access to one at all times)

6. In school or have a good paying job

7. Funny

8. Goes to church (at least on Easter)

9. A little rough around the edges

Lillian Prince

19

I was 19 years old and working as a teller at Bank of America when I met Tony. The fact that I was employed there was so ironic, considering that Bank of America had hit me with every thirty-five-dollar overdraft fee possible since I'd opened my first checking account. Thanks to their no-BS-with-a-smile policies and my poor money management skills in college, I'd eaten more thirty-seven-dollar Snicker bars and forty-three dollar Happy Meals than I'd like to admit. Obviously, you didn't have to know how to handle your own money to count theirs.

While minding my business at work one day, a sexy, stocky, espresso-hued gentleman saunters up to my window. He was muscular, but a little on the short side (think Kevin Hart-ish). Despite not meeting my typical height requirement, there was something about him I found attractive. I noted on my *Must Haves* list that he had to be "tall", but I actually meant he just had to be tall-er than me. I'm 5'2 so this wasn't normally a hard requirement to fill.

"You aiight?" he asked.

Interesting greeting, but I'll go with it.

I was young, dumb, and already impressed with his total disregard for the *l* and the *r* in the word "alright."

"Yes, I'm fine." I smiled. "How can I help you?"

"I need to cash this check from my part-time job."

He put a lot of emphasis on "part time." I guess he was worried that I would think he was living off of this $420 check he was cashing. The dollar amount didn't bother me; I was actually more concerned about why he didn't have direct deposit.

"How would you like this back, umm..." I glanced down at the check, pretending I hadn't already committed his name and street address to memory. "Mr. Tony Greene?"

"With your number."

Oh, that's cute.

I passed him a white envelope with his cash and my phone number.

He called me the next day, and I was immediately reminded of our interaction from the day before.

"Wassup, Slim?"

"Wassup, Beautiful?" would have been a little more endearing, but everything about him was rough around the edges and I loved it.

My teenage imagination started to run wild. I could already picture it. I'd be the innocent, big-hearted, college girl who swoops in and saves the street dude by putting him on the right path. He'd not only get a job with direct deposit, but he'd come home every night by 6:00 for dinner, and we'd curl up together to watch *A Different World* reruns on TV Land.

But first, a date.

That night on the phone we agreed to go to the movies on Friday night. The days between our short conversation and the date flew by. As I got dressed for the evening, I knew one thing for sure—flat boots were my only option. I was one kitten heel away from being Lisa Leslie standing next to Danny DeVito.

Mr. Short and Street (see what I did there?) called me promptly at 8:30, which was the exact time he told me he'd be there to pick me up. *This is a good sign.* Smiling, I picked up the phone.

"Hey, baby. I'm here."

"Are you coming up?" I thought it was obvious that a man should get out of the car and greet a woman at her door for a date. I was slightly annoyed, but I had to remind myself that some guys just needed a little nudge from time to time. Chivalry wasn't necessarily dead, but it did need to be resuscitated every now and then.

"OK. What floor are you on?"

"I'm at the top on the third floor. You'll have to take the stairs. There's no elevator in my building."

"Oh hell nah, I aint walking up all them stairs. I'll just wait down here."

What tha-? The night was starting off on the wrong foot but I was hoping things would get better once we headed out; I grabbed my purse and jacket and made my way to the car. *Be cool, Lillian, be cool.*

I walked outside, and I could hear his music before I spotted his car. The windows vibrated from the bass. In fact, the whole car seemed to thump to its own heartbeat. As I approached his car, I saw him reach over and turn the volume down. I walked to the passenger side and waited on the sidewalk. He looked at me confused.

Pop!

I heard the car door unlock but he didn't move. *So he's not even going to get out and open the door?* Something told me to head right back into my apartment, it wasn't like he was going to chase me up *"all them stairs",* but for some reason I got in anyway.

Tony was completely clueless and after giving me an appreciative once over with his eyes, he threw the car in drive and pulled off. "'Scuse the smell, baby. I let my cousin use the car earlier. I'ont know what he was doing in here."

If I had to guess, I'd say the reason he's going to fail his next random drug test at work.

"So I see all those jokers tryna talk to you at the bank when I'm in there. Who else you been out wit?"

When today? Or in general? I didn't think he'd find any humor in that reply, so I decided it was best to stick with a safe response, also known as a lie.

"No one. You're the first guy I've been out with from the bank." Thankfully his eyes were focused on the road, and he couldn't catch mine rolling in the back of my head.

I could have been wrong, but I picked up on a little possessiveness beneath his playful questions. Maybe I was thinking too much, but I had a feeling this was how Ike and Tina's first date started.

After more uncomfortable and awkward small talk in the car, we finally arrived at the movies. To my surprise, he held the door for me as I walked into the lobby. I don't believe for one second that he was intentionally trying to be a gentleman, I think his real goal was to get a good look at my butt.

As soon as we got inside and headed to the counter to purchase our tickets, I noticed three very attractive and very tall men standing to my right. For a split second, my attention was diverted to the men I'd be able to wear my high heels with. *Hey, a little looking never hurt nobody.* I quickly came out of my gaze and refocused my attention back to my date.

Tony asked me if I wanted anything from the concession stand. As always, I had my heart set on my favorite movie snack.

"Yeah, I think I'll have some nach—"

"Oh, OK! I see these dudes ackin' like they 'on't see me wit' chu! Just like I ain't standing wit' chu! When I bust one off in here I bet they see me then!" He yelled.

OH.

MY.

GAWD.

I liked my guys a "little" rough around the edges, not

full-blown episode of The Wire rough. What just happened? And what does he mean "bust one off" in here? Does he have a gun on him? On another note, what I'm really wondering is which one of those tall guys was checking me out, but I probably shouldn't ask.

My appetite sunk as my embarrassment rose. I knew everybody within fifty feet of us heard his outburst and I did not want to cause any more of a scene.

"Umm, let's just go in the movies." I turned my back to him and started heading towards Theater Eight. He grabbed my elbow before I could get too far.

"You want something to eat or what!?"

Oh, I guess he wants to fight me too.

"No, I just want to go in the movies, please."

I should have replaced "please" with "Foolio," but I knew better. This lil' man, unlike all the other normal men under 5'6 I've dated, was suffering from an extreme case of Napoleon Complex and I had enough sense not to push it. At this point I just wanted to get through the date without having to file a police report at the end of the night.

We found two end seats towards the back of the theater and slipped into them just as the previews were starting. I looked around and saw all of the happy couples, snuggled close together and munching on popcorn. I couldn't help but wonder if any of them would mind giving me a ride home.

I sank deep into my seat and silently prayed for this to be the quickest movie I'd ever seen. I figured we could manage to sit here for an hour or so without Tony having any more ridiculous outbursts. But that was just wishful thinking.

There were two cheerleader-esque, white, teenaged girls seated in front of us. As we watched the film, I noticed that one girl, (we'll call her "Shelly") who sat directly in front of Tony, turned around a few times and threw him an irritated glance. Had I been on a date with a semi-normal person, I would have asked him if he also noticed what she was doing, but I wasn't. I was with a complete nutcase, so I didn't say one word.

Towards the end of the movie Shelly did it again, but this time she whispered, "Can you *please* stop bumping my seat?!?"

I knew at that moment this wasn't going to end well.

Instead of apologizing, Tony yelled, "TURN AROUND, SHUT THE F*CK UP, AND WATCH THE MOVIE!!!"

Ohhhh no. No no no no no. What is happening here?

Still not realizing the danger she was in, Shelly turned around and whisper-yelled, "I AM ONLY TRYING TO WATCH THE MOVIE!"

Shelly, noooooooo. Don't do it, girl. Don't be the hero this time.

That's when Tony lifted up that short leg of his and kicked the back of poor Shelly's seat as if he was trying out for the punter position with the Baltimore Ravens. She literally went flying out of her seat. And I do mean literally. I was stunned.

I wanted to vanish, but there was only one thing left for me to do: Pray.

Lord, please let me disappear. Jesus, if you can hear me, just let me grow wings and fly right outta here!

"Tony?!? What is wrong with you? Why would you kick her seat like that?" For some reason, I was still whisper-yelling as if the entire movie theater wasn't already looking at us.

"'Cuz I know when somebody tryna play me. She keep leaning back all far on my knees tryna be funny."

Lil Man. You MIGHT be 5'4 with double-soled Timbs on. There is absolutely no reason for your knees to even brush the back of her chair. To be honest, if you sat up straight enough, your feet would probably dangle just a little.

I had never been so embarrassed in my life. I was in a despicable situation, and I wanted to get out of there immediately. I stood up, grabbed my leather jacket from the seat, zipped up my purse, swung my hair back like I was Naomi Campbell and said, "That's it! I'm ready to go!"

I had enough. This was crazy and there was no way I was going to sit through another—

"MAN, SIT CHO ASS DOWN. THE MOVIE AIN'T OVER WITH!"

He looked me up and down and then turned back to the screen. He didn't even wait for my response.

So what do you guys think happened next? You're probably thinking I stormed out of that theater, fuming, and hopped in the first taxi I saw, right? No. I actually did what any sane, rational woman who valued her life would do in a similar situation.

I plopped my butt right back in that seat.

As I sat back down, humbled, I whispered in a much more appropriate tone, "Well, you don't have to be nasty. I'm ready when you are."

The credits were rolling before I even thought about reaching for my jacket again.

Hey, judge me if you please and you can talk all the "Oh, I woulda' did this and that and this and that" trash you want. I was out with a ticking time bomb, and I wanted to make it home in one piece so I could promise my mom that I would only date tall men from here on out.

After Tony gave me the greenlight to go, he got up and started walking down the steps with his chest stuck out. Mr. Short and Street was proud of checking that preteen. I, on the other hand, was sincerely sorry.

I stopped by Shelly's seat on my way out. She was still seated; I'm sure just waiting for the coast to clear. I said, "I'm so sorry." I started to explain, "This is my first date with him. I really had no idea he was off. Are you OK?"

Shelly didn't say one word to me. She just stared at me the same way you would look at a woman that you know is being battered at home.

I caught up with Tony when I walked out of the theater. I'm not 100% sure he would have waited for me if I would have taken two more minutes, which in hindsight probably would have been the best ending to this date.

"Did you enjoy the movie, babe?" he asked as if nothing had happened.

Babe? Really? This dude was certifiably crazy, but two could play this game.

"Yeah, it was cool."

"You wanna go get a bite to eat?" he asked.

There was no way I was going anywhere with him. I had to think fast. "Naaaaah. Actually a couple of my girlfriends are at the diner across the street. I'mma walk over there and meet them."

No they aren't.

"Oh, OK. You want me to come with you?"

Not in a million years.

"Naaaaah. They just want to have some super personal girl talk."

"OK, cool. I'mma call you when I get home."

I'm not gonna answer.

"Sounds good." I smiled sweetly. Giving him a quick church hug, I broke free and walked to the diner across the street as fast as my legs could carry me. I headed straight for the bathroom, locked the door, and called a cab.

Lesson Learned

First and foremost, don't date a man who doesn't have direct deposit. When he walked in that bank and signed the back of his payroll check in the year 2000 and anything, I should have known right then that something wasn't right.

But at that time, a little muscle and a few compliments went a long way. And what can I say, what I thought was cute and excused as "rough around the edges" was actually rudeness mixed with little-to-no home training. There was absolutely no need for a second date after a first one as awful as this one.

20

I was 20 years old when I decided to invite Thomas to my company's annual holiday party. He was in my Creative Writing class and we'd been exchanging smiles and flirting with each other since the first day we met. He was smart and well-spoken and he wasn't too bad on the eyes either. My co-workers had raved so much about how nice and swanky the bank's parties were that I finally decided to go, and there was no way I was showing up alone.

After our Monday evening class, I stopped Thomas in the hall to invite him to the party. He didn't even try to play it cool. He said, "Yes" before I could get the question out.

"Do you have a suit?" I asked.

"Yep, but I might go buy a new one."

I laughed. "You don't have to do that."

"Yes I do." He replied.

He was being a little extra, but I appreciated it.

"What time should I pick you up?" he asked.

"7:00"

"OK, cool, I'll see you Friday. Text me your address!" He beamed all the way out of the building.

Thomas was definitely excited, and I had to admit, so was I. It had been a while since I'd been out with a guy I truly liked, so I was sort of curious to see where our first date might lead. When the night of the party came around, I chose a long, fitted, black dress and black heels. My hair was pulled back in a bun and I wore just the right amount of makeup. I looked forward to my co-workers seeing me all dressed up. This was a nice change from the basic slacks and button ups I wore to work every day.

My phone rang at 7:00. Thomas let me know that he was downstairs, and he insisted on walking up the three flights of stairs to my apartment to meet me at my door. I told him he didn't have to since we were already pressed for time, but he said he wanted to be a perfect gentleman.

I greeted him at the door with a smile and immediately noticed how handsome he looked in his suit. He was even cuter than usual outside of the typical jeans and sweatshirts he wore to class. He reached out to hug me, and when I stepped towards him, something hit me.

This man is musty.

Thomas' eyes were fixated on me, so I tried not to allow my thoughts to show up all over my face as they often did. My natural instinct was to wrinkle my nose in an attempt to guard my nostrils from the smell, but I couldn't do that right to his face. The odor that crept from his body was a mix of onions and day-old sweat.

The dab of cologne on top was fighting a losing battle.

I stood at arm's length from him, trying to put enough distance between us to not give away my true thoughts.

How could this be? There's no way he showered before he got dressed. Hell, there's no way he showered this week. It's December for goodness sake. I could almost understand this if it was in the middle of summer, and he had just finished running the last leg of the 4x1 relay in ninety-seven degree weather, but it's cold outside. He also has on a coat and I can smell him through layers of clothes!

Thomas sensed the awkwardness of the moment and my distance so he interrupted my thoughts.

"You OK?"

I didn't realize it, but I had completely spaced out for a moment, or maybe I had temporarily blacked out from the smell.

My mind raced with scenarios to try to give him the benefit of the doubt. I came to the quick conclusion that Thomas had either cooked a steak and cheese with extra onions and garlic right before he left the house, or he had just finished a very intense game of thirty-three with his friends moments before picking me up. I wondered which one it was so I decided to do a little interrogation.

"Have you eaten today?" I asked him.

"Nah. I had a huge breakfast earlier. I'm starving."

OK, so he didn't just cook.

"Did you do anything fun after class?" *Like run a marathon, climb a tree...anything?*

"Nah, I went and picked my suit up from the tailor, took a shower, and got dressed."

Took a shower? Oh, you need to go see a doctor. Immediately.

I held out one last piece of hope. *Could it have been the steps? Those three flights are pretty steep.*

I was almost scared to walk back downstairs out of fear that they might have the same effect on me. I couldn't chance both of us walking out of here smelling bad.

"You ready to go? I don't want to make you late. You look too beautiful to be late," he said.

He was such a nice guy, minus his BO. We headed down the steps and hopped in his truck, which smelled equally as bad. I couldn't believe I was headed to the classiest event of my life with a smelly date. I had to text my girlfriend Jillian, who also had class with us.

Me: Jill. He STINKS.

J: Even tonight?

Me: *confused emoji* what do you mean "even tonight?" Have you smelled him before?

J: Yeah, I smelled him one day in class.

Me: What do you mean you smelled him one day in class!??!! Why you ain't say something when I told you I was bringing him tonight??!?

J: I thought I told you!

Me: Jill… you thought you told me he smelled like day-old trash and I said, "Oh, that's cool. I'll still go out with him"

No response.

Me: HELLO?!?!

J: Oh, my bad, I'm watching Girlfriends. *Joan is hilarious.*

Me: JILLIAN!!!! I'm out with a human dumpster right now and you're in the house talkin' about, "I thought I told you." I'm so mad with you!!!!!!

J: LOL! I'm sorry. I really thought I told you. I honestly thought you knew.

Me: Bye, Jillian.

As Thomas and I rode to the party, we exchanged very few words. I discouraged a lot of small talk because my mind was entirely focused on how I would get through the rest of the night. If any of my co-workers caught a whiff of him, I'd be the laughing stock of the breakroom for the foreseeable future. Luckily for me this was a pretty huge event, and employees from all over our region would be there. So there was a very good chance I wouldn't see anyone from my branch anyway.

Please, God. Don't let me see anyone I know.

Thomas pulled up to the front of the hotel.

"I'll let you out here so you don't have to walk. I'll go park and meet you inside."

Why did he have to be so sweet? This would be much easier to handle if he was a jerk, but Thomas was a really nice guy with a really serious hygiene issue. I couldn't look past his body odor even if I wanted to, but there wasn't much I could do about it that night. We were already at the party, so I had to make the best of it.

I stood at the door, with my coat on and my purse on my shoulder as if I was ready to walk right back outside. Thomas made his way in from the parking lot and as soon as he stepped inside, he headed for the coat check in the lobby.

I didn't move.

"Where are you going?" I asked.

Thomas looked at me, puzzled. "Don't you want to check your coat?"

Nah. If you're on ten with the jacket on there's no way I'm letting you take it off.

"It'll probably be cold inside, so let's just keep them on for now." I said.

"You sure?"

I've never been surer about anything in my life.

I just nodded. I could tell he was confused, but he didn't press the issue. Placing his hand on the small of my back, Thomas escorted me inside the ballroom.

The party was already in full swing. There was an open bar and waiters walking around with trays of passed hors d'oeuvres as we made our way through the room. My co-workers were definitely on point with this one. This event was officially the fanciest thing I'd ever attended without my parents.

We walked around a bit to check the place out. Along the way, at least three people, who were just trying to be helpful, stopped us to ask if we knew about the coat check. I guess we did look a little weird walking around with our coats on, but if they only knew what was brewing beneath Thomas' jacket, they would understand. I wanted to tell them all, "Listen, I'm just looking out for you."

Instead, I always responded with a smile and a polite, "Yes, we know, thank you. But we're just trying to stay warm." For effect, I would run my hands up and down my arms to convince them just how cold I was. It sounded stupid in my head and even worse when it actually came out of my mouth, but it was the only hope I had of my date not setting off a smoke alarm in here. This boy was on FIYAH.

The best case scenario would be to grab a seat somewhere, in the dark, and hide out from anyone I might know. My eyes scanned the room for a spot, but before I could find a cozy corner for us to duck into for rest of the night, I heard someone call out my name.

"Lillian! Lillian!"

The room was fairly dim, but I knew exactly who the shrill voice belonged to. It was my nosey, outspoken co-worker, Margaret. She had an opinion about everything from Friday doughnuts in the breakroom to whose skirt was too short for the teller line. She was the absolute last person I wanted or needed to see. I refused to look up, hoping she'd get the hint. If I ignored her long enough, maybe she would just go away and Thomas wouldn't notice.

"I think that lady is calling you," Thomas said.

So much for that.

"No, I don't think so. I think she's saying Jillian."

In an instant, Meddling Margaret was headed our way. My heart was about to pop out of my chest as she started walking toward us.

"Hey, girl! You didn't see me. I was trying to get your attention. We saved you a seat."

Ugh! You are so nerve wracking!

I cracked a fake smile. "Oh no, you didn't have to do that."

I really wish you wouldn't have.

"Plus I have my date with me."

Margaret playfully swatted me on the arm. "Girl, we saved him a seat, too. We knew you were bringing someone." Now that she was closer, she gave Thomas a quick up and down to check him out. I could hear her brain collecting and computing data like a robot. The more information she could gather, the better.

At this point I had no other choice but to introduce them. Cue the fake smile again.

"Thomas, this is Margaret. Margaret, this is my friend, Thomas."

She extended her hand to shake his. Margaret's face contoured into that classic, "what's that smell" expression and she started to sniff the air around her. I saw it all over her face.

Please Margaret, just don't...

"Y 'all smell that?"

Why is she doing this?

I pretended I had no idea what she was talking about. I answered quickly. "Hmm. No."

She wouldn't let up. "You don't smell that?"

She began to look all around, even checking the bottom of her shoe as if there was a possibility that she had stepped in cow dung while walking over to us.

Thomas interjected, "I don't smell anything."

Because it's you. It's in your pores, Thomas.

I shyly laughed it off. "Girl maybe it's the food. Umm, where's the table?" I had to divert her attention before she caused a real scene. The sooner we got away from her, the better. A true drama queen, Margaret was one of those people that even if she did realize it was him, she would continue to badger any and every one we passed. I could hear her now. "Do y 'all smell that? Come over here, do you smell it now?" I needed to give her something else to focus on.

She let it go for a second and motioned for us to walk with her as she headed towards our table. "Follow me." She led us right to our seats that were just a few feet from the dance floor.

"Oh, this is perfect. We can leave our jackets here and go dance," Thomas said.

I'd rather fake a full-blown asthma attack than allow this man to take his coat off and possibly work up a sweat to go on top of whatever I already smell.

Since I didn't know how to induce respiratory arrest or something similar, I went with my next best option.

"Oh no, I think my cycle just came on. Excuse me for a second."

I glanced at Thomas briefly enough to see a flash of horror on his face. Every woman knew that the mention of the period, or anything related, was a no-no for men. I hated to pull that card, but I was desperate. I ran off to the bathroom and waited there for about ten minutes to make it believable before returning to the table. I conjured up as much distress on my face as possible, based on what I'd learned in my tenth-grade acting class and I went back to the table looking as pitiful and distraught as I could.

"We have to go. I'm so sorry."

Thomas made the "ugh" face before he could catch himself. "You came on?"

Normally his response would have made me feel self-conscious, maybe even a little irritated, but I didn't care what he thought or believed. I just wanted to get out of there. I looked over at Margaret, and I could tell she had a thousand questions. I had no intention of answering any of them. I started heading for the exit before anyone else noticed and Thomas was in tow right behind me.

He went to get the car while I waited in the lobby again. I was committed to my story now, so when he pulled up, I added cramps and a headache to the script to make it authentic.

We rode home in silence. I told Thomas I needed to crack a window to help with my imaginary headache. The winter air was chilly, but there was no way I could have survived a thirty-minute car ride without it. I huddled up in my coat and leaned over toward the window to catch as much fresh air as I possibly could.

Thomas dropped me off at home that night, and we never went out again.

He asked me out a few more times, but after I nicely declined each and every offer, he finally gave up.

Lesson Learned

I guess it could be as simple as don't go on your first date stinkin'. But it was actually a reminder that first impressions are EVERYTHING. You can't show up for the first date, or any date for that matter, smelling bad and expect that you'll get another shot.

I didn't know that I needed to add good hygiene to my Must-Haves List, I thought that was a given, but that night changed my perspective. In all honesty, Thomas was actually a super nice guy. He was well mannered, dressed appropriately for the night, and a perfect gentleman. BUT...I could not sit through another night of holding my breath for minutes at a time and the thought of having to one day have a hygiene talk with a grown man just didn't seem like a fun idea to me. I wished him well but I had to let this one go.

21

I was 21 years old and out grabbing breakfast across the street from my summer job when I met Brandon. I've always been one of those people that dressed according to my mood, which was highly contingent on the weather outside. Unfortunately for me, it was raining on this particular day, and I was in between hair appointments. Plain and simple, I looked bad. I didn't expect to run into anyone I knew, so I wasn't too concerned.

Normally, on a day like this, I would just run back and forth to the vending machine and get ripped off from buying quarter-sized bags of chips for a dollar just to avoid seeing anyone while going to get breakfast or lunch. But when the hunger pangs became too much, I decided to venture out with the intention of dashing back to the office as quickly as I could.

As soon as I walked into the deli, I noticed this cute guy who I'd seen on campus at Morgan State. I knew it was him because he had beautiful, long dreadlocks that almost hit his waist. I could spot them a mile away. I always thought he was handsome, but since he never made a move, I didn't either, and today definitely wasn't the time to do so since I wasn't at my best.

I did everything I could to remain incognito. I slipped to the back of the store, purposely staying next to the deep freezer with my back facing the line so that he couldn't see me. Distracted from my growling stomach, I quickly grabbed a bottle of apple juice.

Of course, on this day, the line was moving extremely slow and I had been holding that juice about four minutes longer than Mr. Kim, the owner of the deli, liked.

"You buy?"

"Yes, I'm just trying to decide. Thanks."

"You no get sandwich?" Mr. Kim wouldn't let up.

"You no get sandwich today?" he asked again.

Maybe I was paranoid since I didn't want to be noticed, but in my mind Mr. Kim was yelling at me.

"Yep, just tryna decide between the apple or the orange juice before I order my sandwich.

"You always buy apple. Why change today?"

Because I'm trying to avoid being seen by the cute guy that's waiting in line. I turned around to see if he was still there.

He was. And he was looking right at me.

He waved.

I waved back and rushed to the line to place my sandwich order. I hoped that by the time I turned around again, he would be gone. Well, seven minutes and one turkey sandwich later, he was still standing right there.

Lillian Prince

Waiting for me.

"Hey, you work around here?" he asked.

"Yep, I work in the building right there." I pointed across the street.

"My name is Brandon, by the way. I used to see you on campus all the time."

I pretended that this was my first time hearing his name but the truth was I'd done a little stalking while we were at Morgan, so I knew his name, major, and relationship status. You know, the basics.

"Nice to meet you, Brandon. I'm Lillian. I gotta get back to work, but are you on Facebook?"

I already knew the answer to that question. Everyone was on Facebook. I wanted to do some damage control on my appearance and my Facebook page is where I kept a carefully chosen collection of my very best pictures.

"Yep."

"OK, cool. What's your last name?"

I know it's Taylor.

"Taylor."

"I'll shoot you a message when I get back to my desk."

I quickly changed my profile picture to an even better one and scanned through some of the older candid shots to make sure they were all OK before I sent him a message. We became Facebook friends that afternoon, and my plan was in motion. We messaged back and forth for a few days before he asked me to go to the movies that Saturday. Of course I said, "Yes."

He picked me up Saturday evening and we talked and laughed the whole way to the theater. Considering we went to the same school, we had a lot in common and knew a lot of the same people. It felt good not having to force our way through any awkward, first-date conversations. We were both relaxed and comfortable. Things were going really well.

We stood in line waiting to purchase our movie tickets and chatted away until the unenthused teenager working behind the glass called us up.

"Next. What movie?"

I spoke up. "Two adults for *Barberhshop 2*." Brandon slid a twenty-dollar bill under the window sill to pay. He rubbed my back and playfully kissed my cheek as we waited. I know we looked like a cute couple as we stood there. Even though we'd just officially met a few days ago, it felt as if we'd known each other forever. I really liked him, and he seemed to be feeling me too.

After our tickets printed, the attendant slipped them under the window. "Would you ladies like anything else?" He looked back and forth between me and Brandon.

I waited a minute for him to correct himself. I figured he had been moving so fast that he wasn't really paying attention. I knew once he slowed down and got a good look at us he would see that there was a man and a wom-

Lillian Prince

an standing in front of him.

There was nothing but silence.

Ladies? He thinks Brandon is a girl? Wait, so does he think we're lesbians? And if so, which one am I? Surely, Brandon is at least the Dominant one here.

Brandon stared the cashier down and didn't say a word. I guess he figured the boy would correct himself if he held his look of death long enough.

NOPE.

Forty-five very uncomfortable seconds later, the cashier hadn't flinched. He was still convinced that Brandon was actually a Brenda.

Somebody had to break the silence so finally I said, "Come on, babe." I grabbed Brandon's hand and pulled him away from the ticket counter.

Maybe I should have called him "bro" instead of "babe" to clear things up.

I don't think the attendant ever caught on to what happened. I'm almost sure I overheard him say, "What's her problem?" to his co-worker as we walked away, and I knew he wasn't talking about me.

Brandon was visibly pissed, and I can't say that I blamed him. He had to be humiliated and offended by the whole ordeal. I mean, who wouldn't be after being emasculated like that in a matter of seconds in front of your date by a snotty-nosed teenager?

Brandon was silent for the rest of the night. I just followed his lead and tried to enjoy the evening. I couldn't even concentrate on the big screen in front of me. I was too busy trying to catch glimpses of Brandon as he watched the movie. I looked at him from head to toe, almost as if I was seeing him for the first time. The closer I looked, the more I began to notice some striking features I hadn't paid attention to before.

His eyelashes were so long, just like the ones I pay for every two weeks.

His skin was so clear and his face was bare. He's one of the few black men I know that can pull off not having any facial hair.

His locs were long and luxurious.

His hands were kinda small, but I'm sure he's capable of dribbling a basketball.

His clothes were kinda fitted, but I don't think he had to jump or squat to get his jeans on.

His shoes were cute and colorful and very possibly the same size as the ones I had on.

It was as if it hit me all at once that this man was much more than handsome. He was beautiful.

I looked down at my Doc Martens and ripped jeans and admitted to myself that this relaxed, yet cute look actually landed me the role of the masculine girlfriend tonight. There was a good chance that I was, indeed, the Dom here.

After the movie, Brandon spent the rest of the night and our entire ride home talking about all things manly.

I entertained him as he shared these tall tales of playing football, shooting dice and fixing cars on the weekends.

<Insert the I-don't-believe-you face here.>

I actually felt bad that he was trying to adapt a new hardcore persona that really wasn't really him at all.

We went out one more time after our first date. I definitely stepped it up a bit and threw on a dress and heels with lipstick to match in an attempt to be—unmistakably—prettier than him. I don't think that ever happened, so I gracefully bowed out of that beauty pageant.

Lesson Learned

The older you get, the more you'll realize the importance of dating a man who's comfortable with who he is. Had he been able to laugh it off, the way I am now, the date could have been salvaged. Unfortunately for the rest of the night, and the next time we went out, Brandon spent the entire time trying to convince me (and probably himself, too) just how manly he was. That got old real quick. It was time to move on.

Lillian Prince

22

I was 22 years old and driving home after work when I met Mekhi. I was having my own personal jam session in the car and I was completely oblivious to the world around me as I stopped at a red light. I happened to glance over to the lane on my left and noticed this handsome man staring back at me. I smiled and bashfully looked away, pretending to get right back into the groove of the song.

He gently tapped his horn, causing me to look over at him again. This time his window was rolled down. He gestured for me to do the same.

He didn't waste any time. "We gotta make this quick! We only have about 45 more seconds until the light changes! What's your number?" He held up his cellphone so that I could see that he was ready to enter the number as I gave it to him.

How is he so sure that I'm going to give him my number?

He sensed my hesitation. "C'mon, baby girl. The light

is about to change. I'm thirty, I'm not married, I got a job, and I want to take you out this weekend. What's your number?"

Oh, that'll do it. Say no more.

"301-555-5555! My name is Lillian!" I blurted out my name and number in just enough time before the light turned green. He winked at me before he sped off.

Not even five minutes later, I got a text from an unknown number.

"By the way, my name is Mekhi. I'll call you later, Beautiful."

I smiled.

A few hours later he did just that.

"Hello, can I speak to Lillian?"

His voice sounded cute on the phone. Much cuter than he did earlier when he was yelling demands from his car to mine.

"This is she. How are you?"

"I'm fine. I just finished helping my son with his homework."

"Oh, OK. Nice. How old is he?"

"He's five. His name is Jayce. Do you have any kids?"

"No, not yet, but I want some one day." I said.

"How old are you? If you don't mind me asking?"

"Twenty-two." I replied.

"Wow, twenty-two and no kids. That's rare these days."

I could have said any age between eighteen and one hundred and he would have given me the exact same response.

"So tell me about yourself. Where do you work, have you ever been married, do you want more kids?" I asked.

"Oh, OK, Detective." He laughed. "Well, I'm an auto mechanic, I definitely want more kids, and yes, I've been married before but it was just a marriage of convenience."

Here we go...

"Marriage of convenience? What's that?" I asked.

"Well, it's a long story."

"I got time."

"I just needed her to marry me so that she couldn't testify against me."

Bruh.

"Testify against you? I'm confused."

"You know it's a law that says your spouse can't be forced to testify against you in court." he explained.

"Yeah, I know that, but what were you being charged with?" I asked.

"Murder One."

Let me give him a second to say, "Sike."

I'll give him three seconds…

"Oh, OK," was all I could come up with. My attempt to sound unfazed failed.

"You OK?" he asked.

Uhh, no, not really, OJ.

"Yeah, I'm fine."

"That was a long time ago, and I've moved on. Hopefully, I can move on with you. I wanna see where this goes." he said.

I'm not sure if he said, "Move on" or "Move in" with me, but both options are frightening.

"True, true." I was viciously shaking my head no, knowing that he couldn't see me on the other end of the phone.

"Umm, are you gonna be free in about 10-15 mins?" I asked.

"Yeah, of course."

"Cool, I'll call you *right* back."

CLICK

In this instance, "I'll call you right back" means I just stored your number as "Murder One" and I won't be answering the phone again.

FYI: If anyone ever puts that much emphasis on "RIGHT back," they have absolutely no intention of calling again.

The End.

Lesson Learned

When someone tells you six hours after meeting them that they may or may not have murdered someone, and the only reason the legal system didn't find them guilty is because they married the key witness in the case, you are NOT supposed to move forward. And to be honest, I don't know if the outcome would have been different had he told me six days or six months later.

Everything about this seemed wrong, so I nipped it in the bud early. I didn't want to know who he may or may not have killed, why he may or may not have killed someone, or when the alleged killing may or may not have taken place. It was absolutely none of my business.

NEXT!

23

I was 23 years old when I was introduced to Alex and normal protocol before any first date was for me to let one of my girlfriends know what was going on. Tonight, it was Tarifa's turn.

T: Plans tonight?

Me: Yeah, I'm going out with the guy Alex that my co-worker set me up with.

T: Oh, that's right!! What's his deal?

Me: I don't know too much other than he's thirty-three, single, no kids, and he's a teacher.

T: You didn't stalk his Facebook page?

Me: Well, duuuh. Of course. But I couldn't find much there either. Everything is private other than his profile pics. He's cute. Looks like he's in shape. I think he plays softball or something with his job's league.

T: Any mutual friends?

Me: Like three randoms. I don't think he grew up around here.

T: Oh, OK. Sounds cool. Where y 'all going?

Me: Just heading down U Street to grab a bite to eat.

T: NICE!! You meeting him there?

Me: No. At his house. Then we're riding together.

T: Flag on the play! You know you are NOT supposed to go to his house on a first date!!

Me: I know, I knowwww. Normally I wouldn't, but my co-worker vouched for him.

T: Hmm. OK, cool... Make sure you txt me afterwards. Let me know how it went.

Me: Will do.

I pulled up to Alex's building at eight o' clock, fifteen minutes after I was supposed to arrive. I'm NEVER on time for anything. I'm not proud of it, but since he told me that he hadn't made reservations anywhere and we were just playing the night by ear I figured I could take my time.

Alex asked me to call him when I was five minutes away so that he could come down and let me in his building. I was still in my car when he walked outside in biker shorts and no shirt.

STRIKE #1.

Where are your clothes, Sir?

I whipped my car into an open space and rolled down the window to ask him if it was OK to park there. (If you're not familiar with the nation's capital, DC cops will ticket you while you're still sitting in your car, wink at you, and then ride off on their Segway singing show tunes.)

I tried to ignore both the ridiculous display of his body and the bulge in his biker shorts. I'm not sure how well I did though considering that he looked pretty amazing. But he should be dressed for our date!

After I parked, he stood at the top of his stairs leading to his building and waited for me to get out of my car so that we could walk in together. He was cuter and shorter in person. Not elf short, just not as tall as his pictures led me to believe. He was probably around five foot six or seven. He had a light caramel complexion, dark brown eyes, and a really cute smile.

"I would hug you, but I'm all sweaty," Alex said with a smile.

But why? Why are you "all sweaty" when I was supposed to be here fifteen minutes ago?

"Oh, no worries," I lied.

He kept talking as we walked to the end of the hallway to his condo. There was a stench in the air.

One of his neighbors must have a dog. Actually, all of his neighbor's must have multiple dogs.

The smell got stronger the closer we got to his place.

"I lost track of time. I just need to take a quick shower and we can get out of here. I got carried away in the gym. You know how it is," he said.

Oh, sir, I have no idea. I had a double cheeseburger with bacon in the car on the way over here.

Alex opened the door to his condo, and when I stepped inside I couldn't believe my eyes. I'm not exaggerating—there were eight little hot dogs running around his 730-square-foot apartment. *(I knew the exact specs because I did a little research when he told me where he lived. Don't judge me.)*

I watched in silence as a pack of small dogs circled our feet barking like crazy.

What the CUSS IS THIS?! (I'm trying to ease up on swearing, so I sometimes replace actual curse words with the word "cuss." It works. Try it out.)

"Oh, you have dogs?" I tried to sound more surprised than disturbed.

"Yeah, these are my babies."

"What kind are they?"

"Long-haired Dachshunds," he said as he looked at his dogs with the same admiration parents look at their newborn babies. "I thought I told you about them."

Trust me, had you told me your place doubled as a kennel, I wouldn't be here right now stepping over shit and puppies. OK, so I exaggerated a bit. Maybe there weren't any feces on the ground, but it definitely smelled like there was, not too long ago, a pile of poop exactly where I was standing.

*So now we're up to **STRIKE #2.***

"I'm going to hop in the shower real quick. Just give me ten minutes. Relax, sit on the couch, and watch some TV."

Dude. What are you going to do with your DOGS!?!?

He must have read my mind.

"Oh! Did you want me to put the dogs up first?"

HELL YEAH!!!!

"Yeah, if it's not too much trouble."

There were two medium-sized cages sitting to the left of the couch. He put four in each cage and headed to the back to take a shower. As soon he was out of sight, all eight of those hounds started howling. They were staring at me going absolutely nuts.

About twenty minutes later, Alex came rushing out of the shower, topless once again. This time with his towel wrapped around his waist.

At some point tonight I hope to see him fully dressed.

He walked over to the cages, opened them, and let the dogs run free again. He headed back to what I assume was his bedroom with all eight dogs running behind him.

Shortly thereafter, he reappeared with a shirt on for the first time that evening. He wore a tan blazer with a white button-up shirt under it, blue jeans, and a nice pair of brown tie-up shoes. I must admit that he looked great. His house reeked, but he was *fine*.

He grabbed his keys and wallet from his kitchen table and headed towards the door. "You ready?" he asked.

"Yep!"

I hopped up from that couch knowing that after sitting for the last forty minutes or so, the smell from the house was undoubtedly in my clothes. It's just like when you go to your mother's house and she's frying a fresh batch of chicken. You know that your hair, clothes, and any leather goods on your person will now also smell like fried chicken.

We got outside and started walking up the block to his car. I didn't know which one was his so I just followed behind him. Seconds later he pulled out his keys and walked me over to his Smart Car.

Sigh.

"These are excellent on gas." He was so proud and beamed almost as bright as he did about his dog babies.

Yes, they're excellent on gas, but I can also fit two in my back pocket.

I listened to him ramble about the benefits of his little automobile as he opened the door for me to get in. From the moment I sat in the passenger seat, I didn't feel safe. I always wondered what was so smart about a car that looked like you should be able to wind it up in the back. God forbid we hit a pothole or a speed bump, I was almost sure the car would fall apart.

Sitting in the car was the closest we had been all night. Since our seats were only about two inches apart, there was really no other option. I could smell his cologne, which was refreshing, and for the first time that evening I had some hope that the night wouldn't be so bad after all.

We found a parking space after circling the block a few times, and headed into the famous Ben's Chili Bowl. A show must have just ended at the Lincoln Theater next door because the line to get inside the restaurant was wrapped around the building. I was surprised when Alex grabbed my hand and started moving towards the door.

"I know the owner. He saved us a table."

We walked past the long line and a cute, older, Ethiopian lady greeted both of us.

"Hey, Alex!

She turned to me. "Hey Cutie! Your table is right over here." She pointed to a table in the back, handed us two menus, and walked off.

Before heading to the table, I decided to run to the restroom. "Alex, I'm going to wash my hands, I'll be right back."

I followed the signs to the bathroom downstairs and couldn't whip out my phone fast enough to text Tarifa.

Me: Hey! I couldn't txt earlier. He's umm...

T: Umm what?????

Me: Well he has eight long-haired Dachshunds...

T: Eight WHAT? Dachshunds? I don't know what that is.

Me: Dogs! The little ones that look like hotdogs. They're called Dachshunds.

T: WHAAAT?!? (I'm not convinced that's how you

spell it.)

Me: LOL! It is! I just looked it up. Anyway!! That's weird, right?

T: Is it weird???? I wish you could see my face right now. Do you really have to ask that? Is he selling them or something?

Me: Nope, they're all his "babies." All eight.

T: What grown-ass man has one let alone eight LONG-HAIRED DODSONS!! (I think that's the actual spelling... that's what I'm going with)

Me: The kind of guy that's upstairs waiting for me to get back to the table! LOL. I'll call you when I get home.

T: Also, you should cuss your co-worker out first thing Monday morning. LOL!

I walked back upstairs and, as soon as I sat down, I heard the words that would literally cause STEAM to come out of my ears.

"I went ahead and ordered for you. A turkey burger... with EV-ER-Y-THING on it."

It was as if the words came out in slow motion.

WHHHHHHHHHHHHHHHHHHHHHHHHHHAAAAAATT TTTTTTTTTTTTTT!!!!!!!!??????????

Why on God's Green Earth would you order for me? And a turkey burger?! Where's my SWINE!? And EV-ERYTHING?!?! DUDE! Are you kidding me!!! You don't know if I have food allergies! I HATE MUSTARD. I HATE TOMATOES. I HATE PICKLES. And if ANY of

Lillian Prince

*the three are included on this Everything Burger you or-
dered for me I'm going to lose it!!!!!!*

STRIKE #3.

"A turkey burger?" I asked.

"Yeah, that's all I eat."

Right. All YOU eat. What does that have to do with me?

I sat in silence. I was irritated, hungry, very possibly
smelling like eight dogs, and questioning why I didn't
turn around and leave when The Shirtless Muscle Man
first walked me into his box- sized kennel of an apartment an hour ago.

The waitress came back to the table with two turkey
burgers with everything on them, two orders of fries, and
one Diet Coke.

*I'm not sure if you all remember, but there are two of us
at this table. She has one Diet Coke.*

I asked Alex, "Where's my drink?"

"I wasn't sure what you wanted."

*So let me get this straight. You just couldn't bring your-
self to make an assumption on my drink order, which
would take all of two seconds to swap out if I didn't like
it. But my meal, on the other hand, you thought the turkey burger was a sure shot?*

"I'll take a Sprite, please."

The waitress giggled. I think she sensed my 'tude.

After picking off the tomatoes and pickles, and scraping off as much mustard as possible, I tried to enjoy my sandwich while pretending Alex wasn't there. For a brief moment, I actually forgot he was sitting across from me.

When the waitress sat the bill on the table, Alex immediately started patting his pockets as if he forgot something.

"Aye, can you cover this? I just realized I grabbed the wrong wallet. I'll pay you when we get back to my place."

I officially hate you.

Without saying a word I looked at the receipt that the waitress left and then reached in my purse to grab my debit card. He stopped me.

"Oh, they only take cash. But there's an ATM at the front, when you first walk in. Sucks right? Super inconvenient."

SHUT THE F---

I got up from the table and headed to the ATM. If I had driven my car, I would have walked right through the entrance. But since I rode with him in his Power Wheels, I had no choice but to withdraw forty dollars to take this inconsiderate, cocky, puppy hording, pain-in-the-ass out on a date.

I walked back from the ATM and placed the money on the table. Alex snatched up the two bills, along with the receipt, and waved the waitress over. He handed it to her when she got to the table.

"It's all here. Keep the change," he said.

This guy wants me to cut him.

Now don't get me wrong, I was definitely going to tip this young lady. But fifteen dollars? NAH. And he's really pretending that this is his money.

After the waitress walked off with her hefty tip, I headed for the exit and Alex was unfortunately right behind me.

"Where do you wanna go next?" he asked.

"Home."

"Seriously? It's still early."

Do you think this is going well?

"Yeah, I'm pretty tired. We can just head back to your place." I said.

The ride home was much like dinner—quiet. When we pulled back on his street, he started looking around for somewhere to park.

"You can have my space when I pull out." I said.

And you'll have plenty of room because I have a grown-up sized car.

"You're not coming in?" he asked.

"Why on earth would I?" My inner thoughts slipped out before I could catch them. *Oops.*

"You didn't have a good time? Is it about the money? I said I would pay you back." He sounded surprised and annoyed at the same time.

Sir, that was just one of several offenses tonight.

I didn't really think he wanted an answer so I moved right along, "So, yeah. Thanks …"

I couldn't say for dinner because I just paid for that. I didn't want to say for the ride because I would have felt safer on a tricycle on I-95 during rush hour. So I just left it at "thanks."

It finally occurred to him that I didn't have a great time after all.

He double parked his car next to mine. "Wait right here. Let me run inside and get your money."

Normally I would have said, "Don't worry about it," but I had taken one too many losses that night to let this one slide.

I stood beside my car while I waited for him to return. Less than five minutes later, he was back and handed me three five-dollar bills. I looked from the money and back to him, confused.

"I left forty dollars for the bill and tip."

"Mine was fifteen dollars." He said matter-of-factly.

This mothercusser!!

I didn't say one word. I just backed away slowly, turned around, and got in my car. Thoughts of running both him and his matchbox car over ran through my mind, but landing a role on *Snapped* just didn't seem worth it. Just as I hopped in my car, I got a text from Tarifa.

T: How's it going? Still out?

Me: Nope—and let me just give you a quick rundown.

He ordered me a turkey burger with everything on it.

He drives a Smart Car.

He left his wallet at home but assured me he would pay me back when we got back to his place.

And He just gave me fifteen dollars to cover his food. Not the whole bill.

T: NOOOOOOOOOOOOOOOO! You knew he wasn't right when you saw all those dogs. So you're headed home now?

Me: Nah, headed to my co-worker's house to punch her in the throat!

Lesson Learned

Ladies! Trust your instincts! There were a number of red flags waving all throughout the night. It started when he greeted me outside with no shirt on and walked me into his house with eight little hotdogs running around. I should have ended the date then, but what did I do? I continued on as if any of those things were normal. He got me good with the fifteen dollars for his food at the end of the night, but I wasn't surprised. He had been a jerk for most of the evening (i.e., ordering my meal, NOT getting me a drink, and acting like he paid for the bill when the waitress came). I'm sure he decided he wasn't paying for my food when he realized I wasn't coming in after the date. He exhibited every imaginable trait of a jerk and in the famous words of Maya Angelou, "When someone shows you who they are, believe them."

If only Uber had been around then, I would have walked right past that ATM machine and headed straight home.

24

I was 24 years old and had been dating Zach for about six weeks when he invited me to his house for dinner. He was a handsome guy, standing at about six feet tall, with chocolate brown skin. He wore his hair cut close. Very close. Like he knew he was two bus stops away from going bald but he still wasn't ready to go all in. He was confident, charming, and someone I wanted to get to know.

The day we met, I had just finished having lunch with my co-workers and was headed back to my office when I locked eyes with this handsome gentleman. He quickly crossed the street to give me his business card.

Zachary Dawkins, Law Clerk on Capitol Hill

We exchanged numbers and from that day on we met for lunch or dinner at least two to three times a week. We also walked to and from the Metro together every day before and after work.

Zach and I would normally just meet at his place before we headed out for dinner since he lived in the city and it was convenient. But one afternoon, he texted me to change our usual weeknight dinner plans. He asked if we could just "chill" at his house because he wanted to cook dinner. I was excited that he planned a romantic evening at home for us, so I agreed.

I arrived at his apartment around 8:00. I tried to dress cute and comfortable for the evening, so I wore a fitted jean shirt with fitted high-waist jeans. (The kind that made me look like I paid good money to have my waist snatched.) I was READY...for dinner.

Zach opened the door wearing a tank top and sweatpants, with a dishtowel draped across his shoulder. He leaned down to kiss me and grabbed the bottle of wine I had in my hand. I followed him into the kitchen and noticed the table was already set with candles and beautiful flowers.

He's so sweet.

"So what are you in here cooking?" I asked.

"I kept it kinda simple. We'll start with a chicken Caesar salad, then we'll have homemade steak and cheese eggrolls, followed by shrimp scampi over noodles for our entrée, and since I'm not much of a baker, I picked up those vanilla bean cupcakes from the Red Velvet shop you like so much."

He smiled and kissed my cheek as my face lit up.

"Aww, babe. You're so thoughtful."

"You can go sit at the table. It's almost done," he said.

"Do you need help with anything?" I asked.

"Nope. Just go relax. I got you."

I sat at the table twiddling my thumbs and figured this would be a good time to check in with my girl, Lish.

Me: Hey Girly. Everything is going great!

L: What did he cook?

Before I could respond, Zach reappeared with two plates in his hands and he sat one in front of me. We said grace over our food and began to eat. Everything was delicious. From the chicken Caesar salad to the shrimp scampi over noodles, I literally ate everything he set before me. It was perfect. The only thing better than the food was our conversation. We talked about everything from politics to ratchet TV to our families.

After finishing my meal, I dove right into the cupcakes. I had already eaten one and just as I was about to go to work on cupcake number two, it happened.

My stomach politely said, "Not so. Not tonight. Not ever."

Against my better judgment, I took one bite of the cupcake, since I had already grabbed it and I didn't want him to think something was wrong. I sat it back in the box immediately after.

Now, in my mind, six weeks is way too soon for the situation that's churning in my stomach. In a perfect world we would have been married with kids before he realized that I wasn't just made of sugar and spice and everything nice.

"You full? You don't want it?"

Oh Gawd, he noticed.

"Yeah, but I don't want to overdo it."

He headed over to the couch with the bottle of wine I brought over and two glasses.

"Come watch a movie with me."

We all know what *"watch a movie with me"* means. Cue Marvin Gaye's "Let's Get it On." I got up and headed over to the couch and three steps in, it was as if my stomach jumped out in front of me and said, *"Oh, you think this is a game?"*

I had to go handle this. "Let me run to the powder room. Second door on the left, right?"

"Yep. Hurry back."

I do not think that is possible.

As soon as I got to the bathroom I locked the door behind me and I said a prayer.

Lord, please. Not here. I promise I'll go home as pure as I was when I walked through those doors. Just please calm my stomach down. Pleeeeeeeeease.

I had to text Lish.

Me: Lish, I have to go to the bathroom.

L: ??? Then Go, Crazy.

Me: You think I have to pee, don't you? It's much, MUCH, more than that.

L: NOOOOOOOOOOOOOOOOOOOOOOOOO!! LIL!

Get out of there NOW!

Me: I can't. I'm already in the bathroom and I don't think I can make it back home.

L: Lil. Listen to me. You HAVE to go home. What do you think it was?

Me: Man, I don't know. Maybe the steak and cheese eggrolls or the shrimp scampi. It could have been the chicken Caesar salad or the cupcakes.

L: Damn! You ate all of that?!?

Me: In hindsight, it probably was too much. But my goodness, I didn't expect my stomach to start doing the Cha Cha Slide.

L: LOLOLOLOLOL!!!

Me: LISH! Don't laugh! I'm tempted to pull the fire alarm! But then he'd probably try to wait for me and I'd have to yell from the bathroom "No! Save yourself!!"

L: I am literally in tears right now. LOL!

Me: So am I.

For the next twenty minutes, as sweat dripped off my face, I wondered what exactly was in that shrimp scampi. Clearly he had mistaken rat poisoning for pepper, or maybe the milk he used was spoiled. Maybe it was the cupcake. Maybe, just maybe, he dropped the steak and cheese eggrolls in the trash by accident, pulled them out, wiped them on the bottom of his shoe after he came in from a rainstorm, and then fried them. I don't know. All I *did know* was that this was the most embarrassing moment of my life and there was only one thing that could have made it worse.

The toilet wouldn't flush.

JEEEEESUSSSSSSSSSSSSSSSSSSSS! This can't be life. What have I ever done so bad to deserve this?

Perhaps the night could have been salvaged with a full flush, a can of Lysol, and three showers, but this? "This is too much," I whispered aloud to myself.

I decided to say one last prayer because obviously the last two got lost in the shuffle. *Dear God, if I have to call him in here with a plunger I'm jumping out of the window. I don't care if he lives on the eighth floor.*

"You OK in there?"

Get away from the door!

"Yeah, I'm good, babe." My voice cracked.

After three more attempts at flushing the toilet, it finally did its one and only job.

I thanked God, and reassured Him that I would hold up my end of the deal. I was going home. I looked in the mirror and the reflection of a defeated woman stared back at me. Clearly I had been through a lot over the last thirty minutes and it showed. My curls had lost their luster. My face was sweaty and flushed. My mascara had run. Life—the shrimp scampi, the steak and cheese eggrolls, and the cupcakes—had all gotten the best of me.

I hope he isn't on the other side of the door expecting me to come out in something sexy. He could very well think I was in here for the last half hour "getting comfortable."

I completely ignored the messages coming through my phone from Lish.

L: Please tell me you got outta there.

L: Are you still in the bathroom?

L: Ask him what was in the scampi.

L: You think he knows what you're doing?

L: I feel so bad for you.

L: Well do you have wipes on you?

L: From 1–10, how bad does the bathroom smell?

As I walked out of the bathroom this was, without a doubt, the worst walk of shame I'd ever taken. Zach was seated back on the couch and the look on his face confirmed what I already knew. I looked bad.

"You good?" He sounded genuinely concerned.

"Yeah, I'm fine. I'mma just head on home."

"You sure? Was it something I cooked?"

I believe it was everything you cooked.

"No, no, no. I'm just not feeling well. I'll text you when I get home."

But you probably won't answer after you walk in your bathroom.

He called me that night to make sure I made it home OK, but we never went out again. I ran into him a couple times while I was out grabbing lunch at work, and we both just kept it cordial. I was still embarrassed and very tempted to run and hide every single time I saw him.

Lesson Learned

Know the importance of a trial plate. A trial plate includes a very small portion of everything so that you can taste it, let it settle, and then both you and your stomach can decide if you want to go back for a full serving. Keep it cute when you're eating at people's houses. Don't do what I did—I didn't pace myself. Had I done a trial plate, I would have known that my body was preparing to reject every single thing I ate that night.

From that point on, if someone wanted to cook for me, we would cook together. I needed to see every ingredient being slipped in my food.

25

I was 25 years old and out for the night with my girl-friend, Cristi when I was reunited with Miles. She'd invited me out to hear a live band play and I was looking forward to a fun evening. The restaurant-turned-club was pretty packed when we got there, but somehow we still managed to find a table for two towards the back. We ordered a couple of drinks, and before I knew it, we were both out of our seats dancing by our table and singing along to all of the band's covers.

I looked over at Cristi. "Can you see the drummer from here? He looks familiar." She didn't recognize him, but I knew I had seen those hazel eyes somewhere before.

They belonged to Miles Washington. We dated very briefly a few years back because he was so inconsistent. He was always cancelling dates at the last minute and constantly replying to text messages hours later with some ridiculous excuse about "What had happened..." I finally got tired of playing cat and mouse games with him so I stopped returning his calls. But looking at his hazel eyes and watching him play those drums caused a quick case of amnesia to set in. All I could remember were the good times. All two of them.

Lillian Prince

When the band took their break, I headed over to the bar to order another drink. I may or may not have intentionally timed it so we would be at the bar at the same time in hopes of striking up a conversation, but if I did, it worked.

He looked over and did a double take. "Lillian?"

I smiled. "Miles?!" I pretended to be just as shocked to see him as he was to see me.

He leaned in to give me a hug. "How have you been? You look good."

I was flattered.

"You too," I said with a smile.

"You're not gonna believe me, but I was just thinking about you" he said.

"You're absolutely right, I don't believe you."

"Don't be like that, babe. What happened with us? I don't even remember why we stopped talking in the first place."

Of course you don't.

He kept going, "Can you hang around for a bit after the show? I wanna catch up."

I gave him a "yeah right" face.

"C'mon, Lillian. I'm a changed man."

Just as I was about to respond, the bartender returned with my tab.

"Oh, John, put hers on mine."

He then turned to me, "I just bought your drinks. Now you *have to* wait for me afterwards." He smiled slyly.

Second to his eyes, his smile was my other favorite feature about him. "Sure, I'm at that table over there." I pointed to my seat where Cristi sat waiting for me to return.

For the next two hours while the band played, I must admit I danced a little cuter than I did during the first half. I added some hands in the air and slow hip movements with random hair flips. I was putting on a show all by myself. I'm not even sure that Miles could see me all the way in the back, but just in case, I was in full show-off mode.

At the end of the night, Miles made his way over to the table. I introduced him to Cristi who promptly excused herself to give us a few minutes to talk alone.

"So what have you been up to? And don't give me that generic "same ol', same ol" answer you like to throw around."

I laughed. "I really don't do much. I work every day, and I hang out with my girls from time to time. I need to be asking you what you've been up to. You still can-celling dates at the last minute and not texting people back?"

Yeah, I went there. Early.

He found it hilarious. "Well, actually Ms. Lillian, no, I'm not still doing that. I was young and playing games back then. I'm tellin' you I'm a changed man now. I just got a promotion at work, I bought a house not that far from here, and I moved my mother in with me. I'm a stand-up guy now."

I was enjoying our conversation as the place started slowly shutting down around us. His bandmates were packing up, the waitresses were clearing the tables, and the crowd had thinned out considerably. It was time for us to head out. I stood up to go grab Cristi so we could head home.

"Wait, you're leaving?" he asked.

"We all are." I said as I looked around at the nearly empty room.

"But I wanna talk some more. Do you want to grab a bite to eat? I know this spot that has the best wings and fries about ten minutes from here."

"I'd love to, but I didn't drive. I rode with Cristi."

"I can take you home."

"No, no, no, that's too much," I said

"For who? Look, you know me. I'm no stranger. I can take you home. You can even give my number and license plate to your friend. You're good. I promise."

I was slightly hesitant at first, but between those hazel eyes and Cristi literally writing down his full name and number and license plate, I was at ease. She and I said our good-byes and I promised to text her later when I got in.

The conversation with Miles at the lounge was brief,

but refreshing. I was excited about our second-round first date. We got in his car and were on our way.

Five minutes into the drive, Miles said out of the blue, "Damn! I think I left my card at the bar. I'm going to stop by my house real quick and grab some cash."

Wait, this feels like a setup. He's just trying to get me to his house. What is this hazel-eyed bandit up to?

I whipped out my phone to text Cristi an update.

Me: Hey, idk about this… he said he has to go to his house to get his money. Left his card at the bar. How far away are you?

C: I'm not far… drop a pin. I'll come back and get you.

Me: OK. Sending as soon as we stop.

About ten minutes later, we pulled up to a beautiful, colonial-style brick home.

"This is it," he said as we pulled into the driveway.

He was absolutely correct. This *was* it. I immediately started fantasizing about living there. I could see myself pulling up into this driveway every day. The house was so amazing I almost forgot that I feared for my life five minutes ago.

I may have forgotten, but Cristi sure didn't. My phone buzzed with a message. I read it quickly.

C: Lillian, txt me. You good? Send the pin drop.

I placed the phone face down in my lap and turned my attention back to Miles and *our* house.

"You wanna come in and see the inside?" he asked.

I know I shouldn't, but...

"Sure!" I blurted it out before I could talk some common sense into myself. Here I was, with a man I hadn't talked to in years, in the middle of the night and headed into his house alone. Everything about this seemed wrong.

Miles and I walked up the driveway and I waited behind him as he unlocked the front door. The house was even more stunning on the inside.

"Wow, this is beautiful." I stood in the foyer, taking it all in. The entire first level was bright, modern, and clearly new. The high ceilings accented with chandeliers were breathtaking. The hardwood floors were sparkling and spotless.

He rushed to turn off the noisy alarm that went off as soon as he opened the door, and then he came and stood beside me as I admired his home.

"How long have you lived here?" I asked.

"A little over a year. I took full advantage of the market crashing and got an excellent deal. I'm truly blessed."

I pulled my phone out of my purse to text Cristi again.

Me: Abort mission. Everything is fine.

C: What?! Girl I'm not messin' with you. I'm goin home. Txt me when you get in.

Miles turned to me. "I'm gonna run and grab my wallet real quick. You can—"

"MILES IS THAT YOU?!?" I heard an elderly voice coming from upstairs.

"Oh sh—," he mumbled under his breath.

I looked over at him, confused.

"Who was th—?"

Before I could finish my question, a light flicked on at the top of the stairs. An older woman appeared in a robe, scarf, and glasses. Even from a distance, I could see she had hazel eyes like Miles, so I knew this had to be his mother.

"Miles, what time is it?" She asked, but it was clear that she already knew the answer.

"One fifteen, ma'am."

This doesn't seem OK.

Her wrath turned to me. "And what is your name, Miss?"

Uh oh.

"Lillian."

"I'm sorry, Lillian, but Miles doesn't have company this late."

Huh? But Miles is thirty-one.

My eyes and mouth were open as wide as her robe that I so desperately wanted her to close.

I could not text Cristi fast enough.

Me: I'm sorry. Come now. Miles is about to get a whippin'. This isn't his house. His mother is not happy. Come get me NOW.

This woman was two seconds from asking for my mother's number so that she could call and let her know that her jezebel of a daughter was coming to her house after one o'clock in the morning on a school night.

I already knew the answer to my next question, but I had to ask Miles anyway. "I thought this was your house?" At this point I just wanted to get him in more trouble.

Momma wasn't having it. "HIS HOUSE? Oh no, sweetie. Miles has a room right upstairs next to mine and his father's."

I'd seen and heard enough. "Uhhh, I'm just gonna wait outside. Cristi is on her way to get me."

Miles was so busy apologizing to his mother that he couldn't even acknowledge my departure. I think he wanted to say more, but he knew his Xbox and cellphone privileges were in jeopardy so he just let me go.

"Ma'am, I'm sorry..." he continued to grovel as his mother kept fussing.

I escorted myself to the door.

"Uhhh, Miles…. Talk to you when you get off punishment."

I closed the door behind me and waited in front of the beautiful brick house, that a few moments before I thought would be my future residence, until Cristi pulled up. The story was too funny for her to be upset about driving back and forth to get me. We laughed the whole way home.

Lesson Learned

Ladies, don't go back in time! Why do we this? Why do we try to rekindle an old flame that didn't work out for very good reasons the first time around? This guy had already shown me years ago that he couldn't be trusted, but I just had to try again anyway. I don't know if it was the hazel eyes or if I got so caught up in his sweet nothings and the possibility of what could have been that I completely disregarded what I already knew. I didn't learn my lesson the first go around, but the second time definitely did the trick.

26

I was 26 years old when I met Sean at a family gathering. He was the nephew of one of my cousin's best friends. After a few days of constant text messaging, he suggested that we go out. He was a cute guy and he was fun to talk to, but I had some reservations about the age difference. I knew my friend Tasha would let me know if I was overreacting or not.

Me: Tasha, he's twenty-one.

T: *sends pic of baby bottle*

Me: See! I'm not going!!

T: LOL! I'm messing with you. You're going to have fun. Just go and enjoy yourself... What does he do?

Me: He's in school.

T: So where y'all going? I hope somewhere cheap.

Me: I know, right. I'm gonna suggest the movies, and I promise I won't get popcorn. LOL.

T: Didn't you say he was cute? What's his name again?

Me: He's an absolute BUN, and his name is Sean.

T: Girl, call him and let him know you want to go... let me know what he says.

About an hour later after talking myself in and out of actually going through with this phone call, I started dialing numbers. Sean answered on the second ring.

"Hello?" His voice sounded very manly. This was the first time we'd actually spoken on the phone and I'm not sure what I expected, but I was pleasantly surprised.

His tone definitely matched his physical appearance. He stood at about six feet five inches tall. He played college football so he had a very muscular build. He was tall, dark, and handsome... and five years younger than me.

"Hey, how are you?" I asked.

"I'm good...I've been waiting for you to call me all day."

Calm down, young man.

"Aww, I don't believe that."

"Well, you should. So what's up? You still tryna hang out?"

Oh, OK. Let's get right to it.

"Sure, I was thinking we could go to the movies."

"Movies?!?" He sounded appalled.

"Uhhh, yeah, the movies. You don't like going to the movies?"

"Nah, not on a first date. We won't really get to talk

and I want to get to know you."

Good comeback. Youngblood might have some sense after all.

He came up with a better suggestion. "Let's grab dinner and catch a movie afterwards, if that's cool."

"OK! You sure?" I was a little concerned about his college pockets being able to afford a date that consisted of not one, but two, activities.

"Yeah, why wouldn't I be sure?"

He sounded a little offended so I backpedaled. "No, I was just asking."

"OK, so what time you want me to pick you up tonight?"

He isn't wasting any time.

"Tonight?! Oh, I thought you wanted to hang out this weekend."

"I don't think I can wait that long."

He's laying it on real thick right now, but I'm enjoying this.

"Well, tonight works for me. I usually get home around 6:00."

"Bet. I'll pick you up at 7:00. Text me your address."

He rang my doorbell around 7:15. I went to the door and there he stood holding a teddy bear. Valentine's Day had just passed and I know I spotted this exact bear at

CVS in the fifty-percent-off pile.

"Aww, thank you so much!"

I followed him out of the door with the teddy bear in one hand and my purse in the other. In the driveway sat a freshly washed, black Cadillac.

This can't be his car, right?

He opened the door for me, and closed it once I was inside comfortably. He walked in front of the car to get in on the driver's side and as I watched him make his way to his side of the car, I was reminded why I agreed to go on this date in the first place. He looked GOOD. His hair was freshly cut and he was dressed in a nice button-up and jeans. I finally let out a sigh of relief. I was happy to be here.

"Go ahead and try it."

Confused by what he said, I asked, "Try what?"

He pointed to my lap. "The bear. Squeeze the hand."

I followed his instructions and the bear began to sing the lyrics to the Rolling Stones classic, "I caaan't get no.... SAAA TIIISSS FAAACTION" all while swinging its head back and forth. It was really cute.

Until it wouldn't stop.

I kept pressing the same paw that got this thing started, hoping to end the hard rock concert, but it just kept going. I could sense Sean's embarrassment for the defective singing bear and he wanted it to end just as badly as I did. He grabbed the stuffed animal and threw it in the back of the car. It landed under my seat, and for the rest of the ride we attempted to talk over the muffled sounds of "Satisfaction."

The steak house was unusually busy for a Wednesday night, but we spotted two seats at the bar. He helped me get settled before taking the stool to my right. The handsome bartender immediately came over to greet us and gave us drink menus.

"Hey, my name is Ron. Let me know if you need anything."

We both began to look over our menus and I tried to get a feel for what he was going to order. I never order anything that costs more than what my date is having, especially when my date is a college student.

"You see something you like?" I asked.

"Not yet, you?"

"I think I'll just get a Sprite."

"You don't want a real drink? A martini or something? he asked.

"Nooo, I think I'll stick with the Sprite," I said, while trying to be modest.

"Oh c'mon, Lillian, enjoy yourself. Seriously, get whatever you like. It's on me."

The bartender returned and asked if we were ready to order.

Sean ordered first. "I'll have a Jack and Coke."

I followed suit. "I'll have a pomegranate martini."

Sean winked at me. "Thank you."

When the bartender came back so we could order our meals, I stalled in an attempt to let Sean go first. I was relieved when he requested the steak that was about $45, so I ordered the pasta. After handing the menus back, we continued to sip our drinks.

"So what do you like to do for fun?" he asked

Ugh, I've really grown to dread these first-date questions. It's all BS. We never tell the truth. We don't admit our real flaws, and in two months during an argument when you bring this stuff back up, you won't even remember what was said.

"I thought you said you weren't the jealous type!?" Well, I lied, so forgive me for figuring out your all your email passwords and setting up my Instagram account to alert me whenever you post and/or like someone's picture.

But you also lied. You said you had a car in the shop. There's never a car. There's never a shop. There's just me picking you up from various bus stops because...

Sorry guys, I had a flashback. Back to the date.

"All the regular stuff. Movies, trying new restaurants, reading, spending time with my family. What about you?" I asked.

"When I'm not at work..."

HE WORKS!

"…I'm normally just training for football season."

"Oh, OK, cool. You'll be a senior this year, right?"

"Yep! Almost done."

See, he might actually be an adult.

"Where do you work?"

"Six Flags. I'm a rollercoaster operator."

… and just like that, he's twelve.

"Oh, OK. Cool."

"Yeah man, I've been doing this for the past four summers."

"That's awesome."

It's not really that awesome, but I have to say something.

Thank goodness he was nice to look at, otherwise sitting here rehashing his summertime tales of the Adventures at Six Flags would make this whole experience quite depressing. The more he talked about his summer job, the more I realized that the age difference was just too much here.

An hour or so later after a delicious dinner and a couple more drinks, Ron, the bartender, brought the bill over and sat it face down near Sean's plate.

We kept talking, and as I sipped the last bit of my martini I saw him grab the receipt out of the corner of my eye. He then reached into his back pocket to retrieve his wallet. He opened it, glanced at the receipt again, and then he paused.

Maybe he's calculating the tip in his head?

Nah.

Finally, after two minutes of me acting like I wasn't aware of what was about to happen, he said, "I don't have enough."

I should have said, "I know," but instead I pretended not to hear him and replied, "What?"

"It's a little more than I expected." he said.

"Let me see." I gestured for him to hand me the bill.

It was $111.43. *This seems about right, considering that after we finished our first drink he INSISTED that we go for round 2!*

"Well how much do you have?" I asked.

"Thirty-two dollars."

"I'm sorry, what?"

This time I really didn't hear him because it sounded like he said he had thirty-two dollars.

"I got thirty-two *dollars* on me."

On you? Because you have a stack of money waiting somewhere else?

"You brought *thirty-two dollars* with you?" I was trying so hard not to sound judgmental and angry, although I felt both of those things at that moment.

Who brings a random and low number like thirty-two dollars on a date with them? Maybe he started the night with forty dollars (which is just as ridiculous as 32), spent eight on that dysfunctional bear that I'm sure is still in the car singing, and that's how we got to the lucky number thirty-two. An even better number would have been 111 to cover this EFFING BILL!!!! Ain't this 'bout a B...

"OK, I'll put up the rest."

I reached in my purse for my debit card, wrapped the receipt, and all thirty-two of his crumpled dollars (OK, I'm exaggerating again, his money wasn't crumpled, but can't you just picture that?) around it and beckoned for Ron to come and take it.

"Just put the rest on the card."

One-hundred dollars later, I walked out of the restaurant with both my pride and Sean in tow behind me.

"I'm so sorry, Lillian. I was just having a good time. I wasn't really paying attention."

Paying attention? You think your attention span is the issue here? You brought $32 dollars with you. We couldn't have SHARED a meal for $32. At the most, you could have ordered one drink, and I could have WATCHED you enjoy it for THIRTY-TWO DOLLARS.

As we got back to his car, he opened the door for me, and I once again heard the Rolling Stones Teddy Bear belting out tunes from the backseat. This time as I watched him walk to the driver's side, he wasn't half as cute or charming as he was three hours and a hundred dollars ago.

"So you still wanna go to the movies?" he asked as he buckled his seatbelt.

Wait, am I his Sugar Mama?

"No, it's late and I don't have any more money."

Shade.

"Well maybe I can just come in when we get back to your place, and watch a movie or something. I really like talking to you."

Get outta' here, kid.

"Nah, it's kinda late and I have to get up early tomorrow morning. I'mma just call it a night." I said.

The Rolling Stones Teddy Bear serenaded us the entire way back to my house. That thing obviously had a fresh set of batteries installed before he purchased it. It was relentless. He could have saved that four dollars on batteries and added it to the bill.

He pulled into my driveway fifteen minutes later and reiterated how much fun he had. Which I'm sure was true, considering he only paid for ¾ of his steak.

He walked me to the door, but not before grabbing that annoying bear and handing it to me. As irritated as I was, I still wanted to be nice. "Thanks again for the bear." I said.

I'm not sure if he even heard me over the singing, but at least I tried to be polite.

He went in for a kiss. I Mutombo-blocked that and he settled for a one-armed, side-by-side, distant cousin hug.

As I walked in the house, I knew that there would never be a second date with this man-baby.

Twenty minutes later I got a text message. It wasn't from him. Even worse, it was from Tasha.

T: Soooooooo how did everything go!?!

Me: Thirty-two.

T: Thirty-two what?

Me: That's how many dollars he thought would cover four drinks, steak, and pasta. Goodnight.

Lesson Learned

So there are two lessons here. First, as I've said before, trust your instincts. I knew better. I knew not to try and seriously date this young man. I also knew not to let him take me to a steak house. I should have insisted that we go to the movies, even though I'm not sure thirty-two dollars would have even covered that.

Second, which is a much bigger, much more important lesson: Ladies, when you're out on these first-dates, and you're assuming that he's going to pay for everything, always be prepared for the worse. Even if he handles the bill, something else could occur, like him telling you he was almost convicted of murder, but he married the only witness to avoid her testimony and you want to hurry up and get out of dodge. Whatever the situation may be, have enough cash on you and that Uber app downloaded just in case you need to flee. Don't ever put yourself in a position where your next move is contingent on whether or not your date is going to act right.

27

I was 27 years old when I met Ian.

"Has it really come to this?"

I was sincerely asking my girlfriend, Jernee, as we sat on her bedroom floor creating my Match.com profile. She typed away, not bothering to ask me for answers to any of the questions to build my account.

"Lil, there's nothing wrong with this. I'm telling you. You're gonna love it."

I seriously doubt that.

"Just give it a chance. What's the worst that can happen? You get to scroll through a list of eligible bachelors who are all just as frustrated as you are with dating."

"The worst? Me meeting someone who lures me to an alley and kidnaps me after dinner."

"How would you get lured to an alley with your grown self?! You act like we're posting your ad on Craigslist."

We both laughed.

Lillian Prince

"They do extensive background checks on these people before posting their profile," she said.

"Girl, stop! No they don't. They scan your credit card for $29.99 and if it's cleared, you're good to go."

"LIL!! Seriously, give it a chance. You even get to select exactly what you're looking for." As she pointed to the computer screen, she said, "See, look. You can pick something casual or something serious."

After a lot of back and forth and what seemed like two thousand very intrusive, and very personal questions later, my profile was up and running.

It didn't take long for me to start getting requests. Some were visible creeps with comb overs, and others I just didn't like because of their blatant attempts at looking cool in pictures. Anyone with shades on inside a building or pointing their index finger at the camera was immediately skipped over.

There was one guy, Ian, who seemed pretty decent. He sent a message saying that he wanted to get to know me, and after inspecting his profile inside and out, both Jernee and I agreed that he was a good match.

He was a God-fearing, gainfully employed, single man, and he was interested in something serious just like I was. We set a date to meet each other for dinner that weekend.

I arrived to the restaurant before he did. I would have preferred to wait for him at the entrance, but our table was ready so the hostess seated me. The ambiance was beautiful. The room was dimly lit and there was a pianist playing about fifty feet from our table. It was so romantic.

But despite the lovely surroundings, as I sat there waiting for Ian, every reason why this was a bad idea started to run through my mind. *What if he doesn't look exactly how he did in his pictures? I mean, sure, I only posted my best three glamour shots on the site, but under certain lights I still look like that girl. What if he's crazy? All of his pictures were headshots, does that mean he's 3 feet tall? That's it, I'm getting outta here.*

Just as I was about to get up and jet from the table, one calming thought crossed my mind out of nowhere: *What if he's perfect?*

In the middle of my internal rambling and before I could decide which voice inside my head was the loudest, a man appeared at my table. I wasn't sure if he was my date because his face was blocked by a dozen balloons.

Slowly, Ian appeared from behind the helium bouquet looking similar, at best, to the photos he'd posted. I immediately wanted to ask him what filter he used on those pictures so that I could step my profile picture game up, but I decided not to.

He poked his head from around the balloons and said, "Surrpprrriiise!" He stood there with a silly, school-boy-grin on his face. I think he was waiting for me to leap up and mirror his excitement.

I was instantly annoyed because I knew I was going to have a field day trying to drive home with twelve balloons in my backseat, but I couldn't just leave the man standing there so I stood up to hug him and to grab the balloon bouquet.

"Hiiii! How are you?" I asked.

"I'm great now that I'm here. These are for you. I hope it's not too much."

It's actually way too much.

He seemed worried as if it just hit him that gifting me with 12 oversized balloons may not have been such a great idea after all.

"Oh, no! These are great! Thank you!"

Once he saw that I appreciated the gesture, relief washed over his face.

We sat down and painfully made our way through small talk. We really didn't have much to say thanks to the excessive questionnaire we filled out to join the site. We'd already answered most of the normal first-date questions.

The waiter came and took our orders. I didn't pick anything crazy or pricey just in case I was going to get stuck with the bill again.

Things weren't really going smoothly, but I was used to the Level Three awkwardness that we were in the midst of after several first-date flops. But even for a first-date flop, this felt unusually painful. I guess Ian sensed it too and in the middle of dead silence at the table, he decided to kick it up a notch.

"So I noticed on the site you said that you were looking for something serious. And I'm so glad that we're already on the same page about things. I think... no, let me tell you this. God spoke to me on the way here and told me you were the *one*."

For what?

He continued, "...and normally, I'm afraid to be this forward, but from the moment I saw your profile, I knew this was right. I knew God had His hand all in this. How do you feel about that?"

I feel like I wanna take the weight off these balloons and fly outta here.

"Oh. Well....umm...I'm ....looking forward to learning more about you."

In other words, I don't know you.

"In due time," he said. "God told me that He was finally granting me the desires of my heart and sending me my wife."

My Man, you've gotta chill. I wish The Big Guy Upstairs woulda told me something before I got here, because Lord knows I would've stayed home.

Thirty minutes and three revelations later, Ian was already asking me what kind of wedding I wanted. I told him I hadn't thought much about it even though the truth was I'd been planning my wedding since I was eight. I knew any indication that I was on board with his plan would probably have led to this guy proposing before dessert.

"So what are you doing tomorrow? I'd love to see you again." The look of hope and anticipation in his eyes was almost heartbreaking. Clearly this guy was looking for love, but he was looking in the wrong direction.

"I'll be deleting my Match.com profile" is what I want-

ed to say, but instead I went with…"Oh, just spending some time with my family."

"I can't wait to meet them. I bet they're great people."

Meet them? Unless you take a pic of me tonight you won't even be seeing me again.

For the rest of the night, I dodged his overly forward advances and tried to stick to sports, politics, and the weather.

After he paid the bill, he walked me outside to my car and wrangled all of the balloons into the backseat.

I thanked him for dinner and promised I would call when I got home, but I guess I didn't move fast enough because he texted me before I made it in the house.

I: Thank you for a wonderful night.

He followed his words with twenty-seven different emojis. There were blue hearts, red hearts, heart eyes, prayer hands, praise hands—just an array of emojis that all screamed "Run the other way!" to me.

For the next couple of weeks, Ian called to continue sharing God's messages for me. I finally stopped answering and he finally stopped calling. But not after assuring me that he would keep me in his prayers.

Lesson Learned

Let me be clear, I love the Lord! I do. But this guy trying to convince me that God had spoken to him about me was as annoying as those chain letters you see on Facebook that say, "Repost if you Love God, and if you don't, you fitna bust hell wide open." (OK, maybe they don't say that, but they certainly allude to it.)

Yes, I was ready to settle down, and I was looking forward to being in a relationship, but not like this. This felt like an arranged marriage. There was nothing romantic or natural about filling out a questionnaire and someone truly believing you just signed up to be their wife because you checked off all the right boxes. I'm not saying online dating doesn't work, it just wasn't for me. I deactivated my Match.com profile immediately and kissed my $29.99 goodbye.

28

I was 28 years old.

So there's a very integral part of my dating life that I wasn't sure if I should share. Although years have passed, and I've since forgiven him for my own personal growth, if I'm going to be completely honest with you, I'm still embarrassed about it. But despite everything that happened, and as awful as this time in my life was, I learned some invaluable lessons—lessons I have to share with the next woman who may be going through the same thing or something similar.

This date, or better yet, relationship, taught me the power of the words that we speak over our lives and how we have to be careful about what we pray for.

You've read about my dates and the real-life moments of just pure nonsense, all of which were only a snippet of what I experienced in my twenties. Like most twenty-somethings, I had this ideal timeline that I placed on my life and, by twenty-eight, I was beginning to feel the pressure.

According to my timeline, I was completely off schedule if I wanted to get married and have kids all before I turned thirty. Here's how it looked in mind:

28: Meet the love of my life and date for the obligatory year and a half to two years.

30: He'll propose. I'll say, "Yes!" We'll have to plan the wedding for at least a year, right? OK...

31: Get married. Get pregnant immediately, preferably on the honeymoon.

32 (almost 33): Baby arrives. Life is complete.

At twenty-eight, I didn't have any viable options for a fiancé. My stringent deadline to have a house, a husband, and kids by thirty wasn't even possible at this point. I was frustrated with dating and sadly considering every first date as the beginning of my Happily Ever After, but it never worked out that way. I was beginning to wonder if I would ever get married and have kids, so I came up with what I thought was a reasonable, not-too-greedy petition to God that I figured He would be open to. My prayers sounded something like this, "*Lord, just send me someone. Just send me a half-decent man, and I'll be happy with that. I'll make it work.*"

I repeated my prayer for a half-decent man jokingly amongst friends, and sincerely whenever I spoke to God about it.

"Send me a half-decent man," became my mantra.

From my lips to God's ears.

I met a guy in the summer of the year I turned twenty-eight. We went out on a few dates and got along pretty well. I wasn't all that crazy about him, but he was decent enough. He was articulate and he had a nice job title that I could throw around at work. I was able to take him to happy hours with friends and dinners with my family, and he was able to blend in well at both.

He wasn't the best dressed, which, was originally in the top five of my Must-Haves List, but time was of the essence. Even though he always managed to buy the most random of all Nikes, that was trivial when looking at the big picture. I was almost thirty, and it was time to reassess my priorities.

It wasn't until I found myself balled up in the corner of the bedroom in our apartment that I realized what my life had become. Mr. Half Decent had wrestled me to the ground to get my cellphone from me because, as he said, "You're not calling anyone this time."

I held onto the phone for dear life. When he realized that I wasn't giving it up, he stormed out of the room as he called me every kind of bitch he could think of. I locked the door behind him, and for the next hour I listened to him as he kicked our bedroom door with all of his might, over and over and over again. When that didn't work, he went to the kitchen, grabbed a knife, and began to saw at the door to get back into the bedroom.

He didn't make it back into the bedroom, so he slept by the front door that night so that I couldn't leave.

I've always heard people say, "I heard the voice of the Lord" and to be quite honest, I never really believed them until that moment. As I sat in my room, crying and praying, I said, "Lord, how did I get here? Please get me out of this."

I heard His voice as clear as day: "But *this* is what you prayed for."

Right there, in that moment as I was crouched on the floor, I immediately remembered my plea for a half-decent man. I remembered all the times I told him that I was leaving and how he would then threaten to commit suicide. I knew if he didn't value his own life there was no way he would spare mine. There was one time, before we moved in together when he broke one of the kitchen chairs and trashed my room as he screamed at me as if I were a child. One of the neighbors heard the commotion and called the police. I didn't press charges even though the officer encouraged me to do so. He never punched me, and I didn't have any bruises or black eyes so in my mind, this wasn't abuse.

I knew I should run away as fast as I possibly could.

But I didn't.

He had shared his issues with me and I was convinced that it was my job to fix them. I felt responsible for his well-being and because of that I can't sit here and lie to you and say, "…And after that night, I left him and never looked back." That's not how it happened. I stayed. It wasn't for much longer after this incident, but I didn't leave right away as I should have, and that alone, speaks volumes about where I was during that time in my life. I started to distance myself from the people closest to me since they all were starting to notice that something wasn't right. They didn't know it was to this degree, but they knew me well enough to know that things weren't going as well as I was pretending.

One Monday morning, after he and I had Sunday dinner at my Mom's house, she sent me an email at work. It was one line, and just three words that completely broke me down.

"Are you OK?"

That was all she needed to know.

I called her, sobbing, and told her everything that had been going on. She told me not to go back. So I didn't.

I left all my furniture, my appliances, my clothes, my jewelry, and my name on the lease. None of that mattered. None of it was worth more than my peace and my happiness.

I'm not sharing this story to make anyone feel sorry for me. I'm sharing this because I know there are countless women in the same situation I was in. A situation where you're not happy, but you're convinced that you can't do any better or for whatever reason you feel that this is what you deserve. As much as I wanted to blame him for everything, some of this was my fault as well. I saw the signs and I purposely ignored them. I had opportunities to leave, but I stayed. I had to take a moment, look in the mirror, and take ownership for where my life was. I had to ask myself, *"Were you really this desperate to meet a deadline that you made up for yourself that you were willing to deal with this? Were you willing to have the life, energy, and happiness completely sucked out of you just so you could have a permanent plus one?"* I was absolutely disgusted with myself.

That relationship, and the aftermath, was truly a wake-up call for me. I thank God every single day that He didn't keep me in the circumstances I prayed for. Honestly, from the moment I walked away from that relationship, I felt a weight had been lifted off my shoulders. For the first time in over a year, I could breathe again. I was free.

The day I walked away from that situation was the real beginning of my Happily Ever After.

lesson learned

You can't "fix" a man and it's not your job to fix his life. As women, I believe we're natural nurturers. We love a project. So when we meet a guy who we believe has potential, and we find out he's broken in any way, we immediately begin the fixing process. We allow him to unload all of his issues, drama, and insecurities on us in hopes of proving our dedication to him while totally disregarding our own wants and needs.

Trying to solve all of a man's problems stems from an insecurity of feeling like fixing a broken man will guarantee his loyalty in return. At least that's how I felt. I knew I wasn't perfect, so I convinced myself that if I just stuck around long enough to see him through whatever he was dealing with that eventually things would get better. Instead, I found myself broken, depleted, and completely drained because I allowed him to suck the very life out of me. Love is supposed to be mutually sacrificial—one for the other. If you are doing all of the work to hold the relationship and your mate together, do some self-reflection and evaluate why you're doing it in the first place.

Also ladies, run at the first sign of abuse. There's no need to stick around to see if it's just a one-time thing, I can tell you that it isn't. I can also assure you that it will get progressively worse. Love and value yourself enough to walk away from anyone that compromises your mental or physical well-being.

*...But when I became a (wo) man, I gave up my child-
ish ways...*

1 Corinthians 13:11 International Standard Version

<u>Twenty-Nine-Year-Old Lillian's Must-Have List</u>

1 Corinthians 13:11 NIV

1. Relationship with God (not just going to church
   and not just going on Easter)

2. Gainfully Employed

3. A Good Person

4. Everything else we can figure out along the way

29

TIMing is Everything

I was 29 years old, completely off schedule of having a husband and kids by 30, and I was completely happy! And I mean a good happy. Work was going great, and I was in the process of buying my first home. I was six months from my 30th birthday, I was single, and I was content.

For the first time in years, I wasn't looking for anyone or anything to complete my life. Most importantly, my peace had been restored, and I was enjoying every bit of it.

Just as I was settling into this newfound happiness and contentment, an interruption came along.

"Call Tim!"

This wasn't the first time Kevin would make this request. Kevin was my girlfriend Jernee's brother-in-law. Kevin and his wife, Johnise, had been together for over ten years, but when they first started dating, they would host game nights at their house. Tim, Kevin's friend, would be there, and we would play against each other in

Spades. Our epic battles always included a lot of trash talking and Tim shadow boxing whenever he was lucky enough to have more than three spades in his hand.

But that was all it was—a little fun and a few laughs whenever we would see each other. There were no side conversations, or winks when no one was looking, and not even a little game of footsie under the table. So I was always amused when Kevin would blurt out, "Call Tim!" as if I ever had Tim's number or any way to contact him.

"Lillian! CALL TIM! He's been asking about you. He saw you in some pics when you went to Bahamas. Y'all must have a mutual friend on Facebook."

That was code for he saw you in a bikini on a beach and he was impressed.

Not only did I not have Tim's number, he was much more than just a phone call away. A few years after we met at game night, Tim left to work in Afghanistan, and he had been overseas for the last six years. I honestly couldn't even think of the last time I'd seen him. I did recall that he was very handsome, funny, and terrible in Spades. But that was about all I remembered. I never got the chance to really know him.

As I was leaving Jernee's house one day, Kevin stopped me again at the door. "Listen, don't miss your blessing. You better call Tim."

This time his words stuck for some reason. So I did what people did in 2013 when they wanted to get to know a person—I followed Tim on Instagram. He followed me back. Immediately.

His page didn't share too much about him other than he

loved to travel, he dressed well, and he was still as cute as I remembered him to be. I couldn't tell if he had a girl-friend based on his page. There were a few ladies here and there, but he always had some super vague caption that gave little to no insight on the relationship between him and whoever he was pictured with. I commented on a post, something random and pointless, just to make sure he saw me. It was a photo of him in Thailand, so I said "Your trip looks amazing! I'm so jealous."

I wasn't sure what the time difference was and if he even checked Instagram on a regular basis, but a couple days later he left a comment under one of my pictures asking me to download an app so we could talk.

He took the bait.

The app turned out to be extremely bootleg. We sent messages for the next week or so that all got delayed. It would take us days, weeks even, to just have a basic con-versation because neither of us got a notification when the other sent a message. That got old really quick, so he eventually asked for my number. I sent it to him, but I wasn't sure he saw the message.

A few months later, I posted on Instagram that I was just three months shy of my 30th birthday, and I had no plans. This was very unusual for me. Every year, since I was sixteen, I've had a party. All of my friends expected a big bash for my thirtieth but for some reason, I wasn't motivated to plan anything that year.

Two hours later, I got a text from a random email ad-dress that said, *"I didn't know you were that young."*

Despite my initial hesitation to respond to some random, and obviously old person texting me, I responded, "Who is this?"

He texted back, *Tim. How are you?*

I smiled.

From that moment on we talked and messaged every single day. All day long. I remember our first FaceTime date and I was just as nervous over FaceTime as I would have been if he was meeting me in person.

Considering how happy I was with being single, I figured that this situation would be perfect. He was too far away for it to get too serious, but he would still be that companionship that I yearned for. We could talk as much as we wanted to, get to know each other in every way except physically, and— maybe, just maybe—when he returned home to the States we could explore something more serious.

Well, exactly one month from that first conversation he had to fly to Dubai to handle some things for work. At this point, despite my original plan for nothing serious, we were already madly in love. We knew it was crazy considering the distance and the fact that we hadn't seen each other in person in close to ten years. But after talking for hours on end, sometimes as long as 8 hours at a time, we both knew we had found something special. We also figured that no one would understand what we had going on, so we kept it to ourselves to avoid a bunch of "*Y 'all are crazy*," from our family and friends.

One week before his trip, Tim called.

"I know this may be asking a lot, but I don't think I can wait another minute to see you. Will you come and meet me in Dubai?"

Dubai? I can't even get these jokers to show up for brunch downtown and this guy wants me to come to Dubai.

I must admit I was extremely nervous. I thought of the worse. *What if we don't like each other in person? What if I get kidnapped at the airport???*

(For some reason, I'm always worried about getting kidnapped, although not one person has ever even reached for me.)

As fate would have it, we had our first real date in Dubai. When I walked through those gates and saw him standing there waiting for me, it was a feeling I cannot even explain. After a fourteen-hour flight, I didn't feel or look my best, but he smiled as soon as he spotted me, rushed over to grab my bags, and walked me right into my Happily Ever After.

Our story proved a number of things to me:

1. **When it's real, and it's right, it'll be easy.** Now, this man was 5,000 miles away. Our being together made no sense. But that didn't matter to either of us. There were no games, no stress, and no *"Is he going to call?* or *"Am I going to hear from him?"* There were no mysterious nights that he "just fell asleep." It was smooth sailing. We both found what we wanted in each other and we cherished it from day one.

2. **A man should be intentional.** You should date a man who lets you know exactly what his plans are for your future and who shows you the exact steps and process it will take to get you there.

3. **You can't rush a man into being ready.** I once read somewhere, probably on a social media post, "You can be the greatest girl in the world, but you'll never be good enough for a man who isn't ready." This is true.

There was a time when men really wouldn't want to take that next step in a relationship if all of their ducks weren't in a row. If a man didn't feel like he brought enough to the table, he certainly wouldn't offer you a seat to join him. Now I know some women get frustrated because to them it sounds like an excuse, but I would rather a man tell me, "I'm not in a good place right now," over a man who's reaching into my back pocket every time I turn around. And honestly, a real man won't even be comfortable with that.

So don't question yourself or why things didn't work out if one year and one relationship later he's headed to the altar. Sometimes it's simply a case of him being in a better place and ready to handle the responsibility of being a husband. His choices have nothing to do with the woman you are.

4. **If he says it's not serious, it isn't.** When a man tells you he's not looking for anything serious, don't think after two months of wining, dining, and slumber parties that his stance has changed. *It hasn't.* And trust me, while most men can never seem to remember anything like birthdays or anniversaries, he will remember the exact day and time that he told you he just wanted to be friends. *"Babe, I told you on November 3rd, when we were watching that Martin marathon and the episode when he went to jail had just went off and I was frying fish in the kitchen around 6:08. I told you then I wasn't looking for anything serious and you said you were cool with that."* This

leads straight into #5.

5. **Never be afraid to say what you want**. I can remember in my early twenties asking a guy, "So what are you looking for?" or "Where is this going?" and he would say, "Oh, I'm just tryna be friends."

(That's weird because you're also trying to spend the night.)

And even though I knew that I wanted much more, I was too afraid of scaring someone away that didn't want me in the first place. So instead of saying how I really felt, I'd respond with, "Yeah, I'm not looking for anything serious either."

LIES.

By the time Tim and I were reconnected, I had been through enough, I had seen enough, and I was comfortable enough with myself to say exactly what I wanted. I remember during our very first conversation, Tim said to me, "Well I don't think I'm going to ever get married. I'm just gonna work overseas and continue to travel. I don't see marriage in the cards for me."

And I replied, "Well, you're off to a good start, you've already seen half the world. Me, on the other hand, I'm not looking to get married tomorrow, but I do know that I want to get married one day. Whoever I'm going to date seriously would have to know that marriage has to at least be an option for us."

Twenty minutes later, during the exact same conversation, he said, "I mean, well, I won't say I'll *never* get married. Maybe I just haven't met the right person that would even make me consider it."

And a year and a half later, in front of our friends and family, he asked me to be his wife.

10 Dates, a few heartbreaks and a lot of tears later... I finally got it right. Every date and every experience noted in this book was simply preparing me for a love that is so kind, and so perfect and so genuine that it can only be sent from above. This is my joy in the morning, my reminder that God loves me, and my true Happily Ever After.

The Finale.

I'm marrying Tim today.

They're calling me and my stepdad out to take that walk down the aisle.

My day is finally here.

My hair and makeup is beautiful, my girls look flawless, and, most importantly, the man of my dreams, that God made just me for me, is waiting for me at the end of the altar.

I hope this book sheds a little light on your dating life and that some of my experiences will give you a new perspective. I made plenty of mistakes and I learned from each and every one of them. That's all I want for you—to learn and to grow. And if some of my shenanigans can help shorten your learning curve just a little bit, then my book is not in vain.

I hope you know that my happy ending and your happy ending may look totally different and that's OK. I wanted a husband and kids. You may want to travel the world, have a fat bank account, and flourish in your business. Hey, you might even want all of the above. Whatever your heart desires, you go for it. Just don't settle for less because you're too afraid to ask for more.

I'll check back in with you and let you know how married life is going. Maybe the next book will be titled, *12 Months Later... After Marriage.*

Gotta go.

Love ya!

Lillian ~~Prince~~ Mitchell

Book Club Questions

1. Share the worst date you've ever been on.

2. What's the difference between settling and compromising?

3. Compare your Must-Haves List from 10 years ago with your current one. How has it changed?

4. Write a letter to your younger self to prepare that girl for her future dating life. Be open and honest about your ups, downs, experiences, and lessons learned.

5. Of all the dates you read about in this book, were there any guys you thought Lillian should have given a second chance? Why?

6. What's the most ridiculous lie a guy has ever told you on a date?

7. And to be fair to the fellas, what's the most ridiculous lie you've ever told a guy on a date?

8. What's the best excuse you've ever used to get out of a date you didn't want to go on?

About the Author:

Lillian Prince Mitchell is a destined storyteller. The Washington DC Metro native fell head over heels with writing as a student journalist when she was offered an opportunity to cover a story for her collegiate newspaper at Morgan State University. Her love of love, combined with her innate curiosities about the intricacies of relationships inspired her to start the acclaimed blog, *"He Say, She Say"* where she shared her insight as the feminine voice and perspective to anonymous submitters. Lillian has also penned for numerous publications, including the Baltimore Afro, Washington Business Journal, and Sister 2 Sister magazine. A newlywed, she recently married the love of her life, Tim, and in December of 2016, she released her debut book, *10 Dates Later*, an honest, hilarious, and heartfelt reflection on dating in her twenties.

When she is not writing or dishing out witty and wise relationship advice, you'll likely find Lillian enjoying a good home cooked meal and a feisty game of Scrabble with her family.

Follow 10 Dates Later on Social Media

Instagram: @mrsmitch2u @10Dates Later

Facebook: 10 Dates Later

Twitter: @10DatesLater

And check out 10DatesLater.com to submit relationship questions to the "Ask Lil" site.

Acknowledgments

Thank you to my 5 Little Heartbeats, my nieces and nephew: Kennedi, Jackson, Brooklynn, Victoria and Hayven for inspiring me to do better simply because I knew you were watching.

Thank you to my amazing Godchildren: Derrick, Jr., Zayla and Ian. I love you so much.

To my unofficial but very official PR team: Sharnikya and Alexis. Thank you for EVERYTHING you did to contribute to the success of this book.

To Kiyana: For giving me honest feedback whenever I needed it the most. You are so appreciated.

To my 7 bridesmaids, my sister Sonja, my favorite girls: Jernee, Alicia, Tasha, Jillian, Cristi and Tarifa. I love you and appreciate each and every one of your friendships. You experienced each and every one of these chapters with me so it was only fitting that you stood with me for the happy ending as well.

To Tokeitha: I honestly can't thank you enough for answering ALL of my questions and helping me so much during this process of writing and publishing my first book. I am so grateful for you.

To my Editors: Stefanie Manns and Leah Lakins. Thank you!

To my cousin Soweto: For the amazing work you did on the website and all the last minute requests you were able to help me with. Thank you!

Thank you to every single friend and family member that spread the word about "10 Dates Later..." whether you passed out cards, told a friend, bought a book, or posted something on social media...whatever you did to ensure the success of this book, I sincerely thank you from the bottom of my heart.